DIFFERENT KINDS
OF LOVE

The Dedalus Press
13 Moyclare Road
Baldoyle
Dublin 13
Ireland

www.dedaluspress.com

ISBN 978 1 906614 51 5

Dedalus Press titles are distributed in the UK by
Central Books, 99 Wallis Road, London E9 5LN
and in North America by Syracuse University Press, Inc.,
621 Skytop Road, Suite 110, Syracuse, New York 13244.

Cover design: Pat Boran

Printed in Ireland by Gemini International Ltd.

The Dedalus Press receives financial assistance from
The Arts Council / An Chomhairle Ealaíon

DIFFERENT KINDS OF LOVE

Stories

LELAND BARDWELL

DEDALUS PRESS
DUBLIN, IRELAND

ACKNOWLEDGEMENTS

The stories in this volume were first published as *Different Kinds of Love,* by Attic Press, Dublin, in 1987. The author wishes to thank all at Attic Press at that time for their interest and support.

Contents

⁀

⁀

The Dove of Peace

THERE'S A HOLE IN MY MEMORY. I've had other holes—unimportant ones—but this one nags, some days almost to torture level. It could be three days or more or it could be weeks. Lately I have felt an urgency to recapture that dark patch. I fear the failing memory of the old, the undignified lapses, the difficulty in distinguishing one decade from another.

Yes, I'm old, arthritic. Some mornings I can barely lift the kettle. All my strength has to be tailored to my boxes. All over the world you'll find them. I have made boxes of every size and shape, every colour and hue. I have made boxes of ash and cedar wood, ebony and elder. I have made boxes inlaid with garnets and coloured glass set in garlands of flowers resembling the wild herbaceous borders of the big house where she and I used to play.

I have fought this dark patch like you'd fight to get out of a nightmare, stitching and restitching till my head swims and the events before and after become even more unyielding. I have gone back to my work saying, What does it matter now? The past is the past. Let sleeping dogs lie.

This morning again I sorted through the old trunk and reread the famous letter. The envelope was addressed to me, Miss Jessica O'Brien, c/o The Ballyronan County Asylum. Inside, dated 12th July 1946, it stated that my father Joseph O'Brien was dead.

Every time I read this letter I relive the exhilaration of those next few days. I was no longer a non-being. It was like a news flash of world importance that you get nowadays on television.

You see this short period I speak of is not my first experience of memory failure. For four long years I had lived in that place with no recollection of what had happened before I went there. All I could recall was the deaf man driving the old Ford, and myself in the back—a bundle of clothes with nothing inside it. And the gates of the Asylum. I always remembered the gates—each individual strut pointed like a spear and the whole welded together with hefty iron cross-bars. The outside of the building also haunted me—the opacity, the height and the great oak door cut into the wall which was opened with a mortice key some eight inches long. And how the smells had hit me that first day—the mixture of urine and sweet powder.

Nor could I forget my first impression of the nurse who strode ahead of me like a man and had a stone-coloured featureless face that threw loops of sentences at me that made no sense but seemed to settle in my brain in strings. At first I was put in a cell with a high-up window the size of a tray through which filtered a shaft of light that barely lit the end of the bed. The bedding consisted of a white cotton cover, two thin blankets and no sheets. That night I discovered the blankets were as coarse as turf and caused sour weals to rise on my skin.

It was about a year later that a nurse casually told me that my mother had died in the same hospital in another ward and did I want to see her body? What mother? I had no mother or father. I had nobody belonging to me. I ate with old women who dribbled and had to be fed. In the exercise hall I was paired off with a harridan who cursed me all the time. This I had come to accept. This was my reality. I was a non-being, homogeneous, as though I were not composed of parts. I called myself a changeling, a moonchild, and when I wasn't eating or sleeping

I paced the ward like all the others, slowly, back and forth, like floating creatures in a massive tank.

But then came the letter. The nurse read it to me as if I were illiterate, and as she read the words *Joseph O'Brien is dead* my whole body underwent a physical change. I had a feeling of freshness, 'young-ness', clarity of mind. I clutched the woman, implored her to repeat the news. With that one sentence she had given me back my past. Every bit of it, that is, except that short period so nearly remembered, so hidden.

Now that I am elderly and crippled, those four years are of a timeless monotony—grey as the food they gave us which we shovelled into our mouths with large tin spoons.

But how I crave to find you, Columbine, in those short hours, Oh Columbine, my Dove of Peace.

It was Jessica who noticed the mother's wandering first. The trailing abstracted movements as she switched from hall to sitting room, from sitting room to kitchen. Columbine didn't notice. Columbine was Daddy's pet. Daddy bought her dresses and brooches and scarves. 'Columbine can charm the birds off the trees,' Daddy said, as he took her on his knee and she settled her pointed face into the lapels of his jacket. No, Columbine didn't notice the mother's pacing, nor the strain in her mouth, nor the anger in her shoulders. She was Columbine, The Dove of Peace—Daddy had chosen the name because the war was over.

The two little girls shared a bedroom. They had a high iron bed each and Jessica used to tell Columbine a story every night. The story wove its way through Columbine's head until she fell into a gentle sleep. From then on Jessica would stare vacantly into the darkness. If she dozed off, she'd wake frequently, sounds of ghostly swishings, perhaps a human sigh or something louder like a withheld yawn would cause knots of terror to gather in her stomach. Yet somehow she knew that she must not call out or make known that she was awake.

If she questioned Columbine in the morning, the latter would only curl up more tightly into her silky morning warmth and say nothing.

Columbine had soft hair, light as lint, which fell each side of her face in madonna curves, while Jessica's hair was thick and dry, held back by kirby grips. But she was light as a fox and in this way she pleased Columbine, who was all movement, all grace.

Jessica was a year younger than her sister and for this reason all her thoughts, actions and mannerisms were directed towards being as exactly as possible a replica of the elder girl. To the extent that sometimes Columbine would feel irritated by the intensity of Jessica's adoration and would try to shake herself away with an angry, 'Don't copy me all the time.'

But mostly their games were wild and secret, beset with the lore and superstition of the countryside, overlaid by their inventiveness and natural savagery. It was only at night time that a strange anomaly manifested itself.

Jessica never quite knew when she found out the cause of her nightly terrors. It was like a gradual growth of the faculties, the inculcation of logic into her childish brain. These nocturnal noises had, after all, a human origin. There were no ghosts, no disembodied spirits, nothing, in fact, to be afraid of. It was only Daddy, who came up to give Columbine a last goodnight kiss, to hold her soft body in his arms, reassure her of his love.

There was a shed at the end of the garden in which junk of all kinds was jettisoned. When rebuffed by Columbine, Jessica would go into this shed, at first to sulk, hoping that Columbine would follow, and then, when this plan didn't work, her own inventiveness took over. One day while in a complicated fantasy of delving amongst the broken furniture and odds and ends, she came upon a bag of tools. A great leather bag, matted with dust, the hasp askew but crammed with the most exciting amalgam of saws, chisels, planes, adzes and such like, keenly edged and in fine condition. At first she just played with the saws, cutting broken chair-legs and the like. Gradually her fascination grew till one day the shapes began to form neatly. She had fashioned her first perfect square. She taught herself how to make tenons and mortices, how to dovetail the wood so that she could fit the squares together. She had made her first box.

She made more and more, boxes of every size and description. She became obsessed. But it was a secret obsession. No one must know about her boxes. Especially Columbine.

If Columbine found out she would only laugh at her. She could imagine what she would say.

'Making boxes? What for? They're useless.'

Meanwhile the mother's pacing grew worse although sometimes she'd stand stock-still and stare. It was uncomfortable, that staring. Also she sometimes stood in an awkward place, like in a doorway or blocking the cooker.

'What is wrong with Mammy?' Jessica asked.

'She's mad. Stone mad.'

'Why is she mad?'

'She's mad because she can't have what she wants.'

'What does she want?'

'Something big, Daddy says.'

'What does that mean?'

'Dunno.'

Out in the shed, Jessica planned. Perhaps she could make her Mammy a big box. A big box so as Mammy could put everything into it. All her boxes were small because the bits of wood she found were seldom more than a few inches long. It was no good. She'd have to buy her Mammy something big. An elephant? Everyone knew that elephants were the biggest things in the world. But she couldn't get her a real elephant because they were all in circuses. She'd have to get her a toy one.

The following day Jessica emptied her savings box and bought her mother a toy elephant.

'Now Mammy, you can imagine that this is a real elephant and that's a big thing.'

Her mother stopped and hit her so hard she spun twice and landed against the table leg.

'Don't ever do that again,' the mother screamed. And she screamed so much others came from the neighbouring house.

Jessica looked up from where she lay, the blood spurting down her chin. There was the woman from next door bending over her muttering, 'Oh dear, the little one is hurt.'

'I'm perfectly all right.' Prim little Jessica got up and ran into the kitchen to wipe the blood from her face.

But because she was bleeding her mother wanted to hit her more. And more. She picked her up, with the two neighbours watching, and shook her and shouted and the hatred ran up and down the stairs and out the back door and into the yard till the father came in and hit the mother and the neighbours ran away.

Some days after that a van came. A white van. And Jessica stood in the hall and watched her mother carrying her suitcase and climbing into the back of the van. Father was there, too. Nobody took any notice of Jessica.

'Where's Mammy gone?'

'To a mad house.'

Now the girls had to grow up fast. They had to cook and do the housework as well as attend school and do their homework. Dirt piled up in odd corners. Smells accumulated. Food rotted and was thrown away. Daddy grew more and more bad tempered. At six o'clock every evening he'd return, his face ravaged from the raw winds, banging his bike through the front door and the kitchen and out into the yard, leaving a cold draught to circle through the house. When it was Columbine's turn to cook, he took pains to praise what dreadful concoction she placed before him, but when it was Jessica's turn he'd cast his plate from him, shouting, 'Do you expect me to eat this muck?' and storm out to the pub.

Although the girls had long since ceased their games of fantasy, they were very close. At night when the wind howled outside they'd strive to get their homework done, helping each other when possible, giggling over the teacher's stupidity and drawing cartoons in their copy-books.

But when it was time to go to bed Jessica's terrible fears intruded on their intimacy. She was never allowed to mention the father's nightly visits. Starched with sleeplessness, she'd lie motionless till he went.

One morning Columbine said she couldn't get up.

'What's the matter?'

'I've got my visitor.'

Jessica looked around. She thought of the nightly shufflings, the yawn-like noises.

'You're going mad, like Mammy. There's no one in the room.'

'I'm not well.'

There was a new smell. A not unpleasant smell but warm and penetrating, ammoniac.

'Should I get the doctor?'

'Good heavens, no!'

Jessica went off to school in a state of bewilderment.

That night, as usual, Daddy came up. He wasn't steady and there was a foul smell on him. All the men in the morning bus smelled like that. This time Jessica was wide awake and for the first time felt a heavy guilt as though she were to blame. To blame for what? Perhaps when she was a baby she had done something wrong, which was why Daddy only loved Columbine. But no. It wasn't only that. It was sorrow. Sorrow you could touch like a coat or extra padding on your body. Please go away, oh please, she wanted to scream. Tears, cooling quickly, gathered round her eyes, ran down her ears, her neck and soaked the pillow. But this time Daddy didn't stay long. With a furious oath he stumbled from the room. Jessica sat up in horror. In a shaft of moonlight she could see Columbine's face like a scallop above the sheets. 'Are you all right?' she managed to ask.

Columbine didn't answer.

Next morning it was the same.

'Are you still sick? Please tell me what's the matter?'

'I'm bleeding. There. Are you happy now?'

'Columbine, darling, why didn't you tell me?'

'Oh go away for God's sake.'

'But you must see the doctor.'

She pulled the bedclothes down. 'There! Look. Blood! Get me a pad from the drawer before you go.'

'These?' Jessica picked up a packet wrapped in blue paper. The torn label read: Six Sanitary Towels.

'Lucky you had these.'

'Wait till it happens to you.'

'Me? This won't happen to me, will it?'

'God, you're an innocent fool.'

'Do you not mind?'

'It means I'm a grown up girl, Daddy says.'

How could she? How could she talk about that to Daddy? Columbine, still laughing, was holding out the used towel.

'Present for you,' she said.

Jessica took the towel and fired it in the waste-paper basket.

It was a year later when Jessica got her first period. She didn't know what to do so she stole the towels from Columbine.

'You can buy your own. Ask Daddy for the money.'

This was out of the question. She cut up rags and washed them out afterwards. Her thighs were roughened from the coarse cloth. Little scabs formed and barely healed from month to month.

About this time a deaf man became a new neighbour. He drove an old blue Ford. Jessica learnt deaf and dumb language on her fingers, hoping that if they made friends he'd take them for drives.

On these excursions the two sisters would sit in the back giggling at all the passers-by. The deaf man talked in loops because he had never heard speech so they laughed at that too. And when they got home at night Daddy was usually in the pub, so they'd sit together by the kitchen stove eating toast and jam and scrawling out their homework till they'd hear the dreaded noises that warned them of his return. At least Jessica dreaded them, Columbine still laughed at her, saying, 'Poor Daddy, he's unhappy.'

'So that's why you let him?'

'Mind your own business. You're supposed to be asleep.'

One morning Columbine told her they were not going on any more rides.

'Why, oh why not?'

'Daddy says we're not to. Unless he comes with us.'

'But he'd be horrible. He'd spoil everything.'

'Not at all. He says we can take a day off tomorrow and go to the sea. For my birthday treat.' It would be Columbine's fifteenth birthday.

When they reached Hunter's Cove with its small beach laid out like a custard-coloured apron, the sun was shining and even Jessica in her excitement—for she loved the sea—forgot her misgivings.

The two girls ran to get undressed and put on their togs. The deaf man built a fire with driftwood to boil the kettle, while Daddy kept pulling the corks out of the bottles of stout he had brought with him. He was a different man, it seemed, not scowling, no, all smiles and little jokes. Even his crusted face looked less abandoned than usual. He had shaved tightly and put on a clean, ribbed shirt and a 'holiday' pullover.

The sisters bobbed up and down in the water and swam way out till they were tired, splashing each other as they trod water.

By the time they were white with cold they raced up the beach, released into gleeful cries like the gulls that circled and fought the wind overhead. Daddy began to chase them and they ran and feinted with him. Suddenly Columbine was sprawled on the sand with Daddy on top of her. He held her fast, his face gone red and powerful like he was killing a German soldier and Columbine's face was wax and her eyes searched around like they'd pop out of her head. Jessica ran to the deaf man, 'Stop him, stop him,' her fingers raced through the alphabet but he was busy and didn't or pretended not to notice. She ran back shouting at her father to get off but he just kept heaving and she could see the sand matting Columbine's hair like cake and her thin elbows red from piercing little holes by her side.

There were shouts from the rocks behind them. People had arrived, picking their way carefully over the crags with their buckets and spades and baskets and towels. Daddy sprang away and faced the sea. Columbine just lay like a corpse newly dragged from the depths.

Jessica knelt beside her. 'Go away. Go away. Pretend you didn't see. You didn't. Oh … God, I'm cold.' She was twisting and turning, looking at Jessica as though she had never seen her before.

Jessica got up, exhilarated. 'Now,' she thought, 'She'll be mine, again. She'll hate him, she'll never let him near her again.' She wandered into the shelter of the rocks, barely noticing that Columbine had joined her. The sea darkened behind them when a cloud blew over the sun and the beach turned from blond to brown and the wind lifted motes of sand that raced over the surface.

As they tried to dress, the towels were torn from their backs exposing their white buttocks, the sand sticking to their thighs as they put on their knickers and their vests and fought with the openings of their dresses. Daddy remained where he was, legs apart, back hunched as though the changing pattern of the waves were his only interest.

All the way home Daddy stared out of the window, silent, and the two girls isolated in the back said nothing. Only the deaf man mouthed his deaf noises—groans, gurgles or belches—while the meadows and wheatfields sped past, interspersed by the odd useless cottage, distant sheep on a hill like lice stuck to a blanket, or the occasional wrinkle of a ploughed field.

The treat was over.

Months passed. The sisters continued to live in sly seclusion. Jessica spent much time in the shed. No one spoke of the absent mother. Every evening their father wheeled his bicycle through the kitchen and out the back door, leaving the inevitable draught behind him.

It was when Columbine was in the bath that Jessica noticed it first. Her sister was lying flat on her back, her chin hooked onto her breastbone, staring at her belly.

'My God! Jessica said. Columbine's stomach was no longer hollow. Like an upturned saucer it seemed to palpitate beneath the water.

'What the hell are you doing in here?'

Jessica went to back out.

'Oh you needn't go. You've seen it now.'

'You're … You're …' Jessica couldn't finish the sentence.

'Yes.'

'Does Daddy know?'

'No. And don't tell anyone.'

'Oh, Columbine, how could …'

'Shut up.'

She rose from the bath and she'd barely stepped out when the vomit came up like a spout and splashed over the edge of the lavatory bowl. Jessica, paralysed, longed to stroke her sister's forehead, to say some words of sympathy, hold her tight, but a wave of distrust from Columbine held her back.

Some weeks later at school, Columbine was called to the headmistress's office. Jessica listened at the door. The head spoke in sepulchral tones.

'Who is the father? You must tell me. So as he can be punished too. God has punished you for your sin and will go on punishing you all the days of your life.' Her sister was sobbing uncontrolledly. 'Speak, child,' the head kept shouting, but Columbine wouldn't or couldn't utter a word. Jessica ached to comfort her, break in and scream the truth at the woman but there wasn't time. Columbine came rushing out, her face the colour of cardboard.

Winter had scaled everything down, the land was brittle with frost. At half-past four the lights in the village were on as the bus snaked in. Their own house, dark with damp, the scuttle of mice their daily welcome. Listlessly they began their evening chores.

Suddenly Columbine crumpled in her sister's arms. 'Oh God, Oh God, Oh God.'

They clung together, the dead stove, the unwashed dishes, the dirty clothes on the floor the only witnesses. The life between them jerked and cavorted.

All that night they planned. Discarded one possibility after another. Should they steal money, run away together, have the baby adopted? In the planning they grew optimistic. They put a chair against the door and huddled together in the same bed.

Some sentences emerged.

'When he touched me there first it tingled. He gave me

presents to hold his thing. I didn't want to but I couldn't stop.'

'I don't understand.'

'You will one day.'

'No. Never. Is that why Mammy went mad?'

'No, no. She was mad first, Daddy says. Always always mad.'

'Poor Mammy.'

'Poor Daddy.'

'I hate him, Columbine. I hate him. You hate him too. Say it.' But she couldn't say it.

'It's my fault, Jessica. He couldn't help it.'

Jessica hugged her sister till she cried out, 'Don't. You're squashing it.'

Jessica was now allowed to attend to her sister, bring her water when she vomited, put compresses on her brow when her head was bad. At school they lurked around together. The head mistress ignored them. Columbine was always in her anorak, her body at an angle to hide the swelling. Jessica felt that she was pregnant too, that she also was shielding the child from prying eyes.

She began to walk as Columbine, take on her habits, just as she had as a small child. They didn't count the months. It would soon be Columbine's sixteenth birthday. Why was that puzzling? Suddenly Jessica realised that the baby had not started that day at the seaside. There must have been times since—other secret times. Times when they both had hidden from her their fury and their pantings. Jessica felt a sickness gathering. From then on her vomit came as frequently as Columbine's. At night when she held her sister, she wondered when they had stopped, did they even still 'do it'? But she knew if she asked she'd be rebuked, called an interfering fool.

It was a clear summer's night—late May or early June. They sat out before going to bed. They were as they had been that first night when they had planned. They had done nothing, time just hurtled over them. Occasionally a bird uttered or a leaf moved. The night gathered in the village, doors closed, lights went on, radios blared. To their left the cattle lowed in Long's field.

Finally they went up to bed, nothing solved, nothing changed.

When Jessica woke up it was dawn, birdsong shattering the air beyond the windows. She stretched her limbs, sat up, the other side of the bed was empty. Perhaps she's in the bathroom? She lay down again. But minutes passed, ten, fifteen. Shocked she sat up again. So this was when they 'did it'? Around dawn? She felt the old paralysis of dread, threw off the bedclothes and thundered into her father's room. She would kill them, kill them both and kill herself afterwards. She pulled the blankets off him, a heavy firedog in her other hand. He was alone, the body moss-green in the early light. He didn't wake even when she yelled, 'Where is she, you pig? Tell me or I'll kill you.'

She ran out, searched the bathroom and all the rooms. Then a new fear screwed into her throat. They had never really considered the actual birth of the baby. It was as if the baby would be born when they decided the time was ready for it. It had never occurred to them to count the months, to get clothes or nappies or a place for it to lie. Hysterical, Jessica tried to count back now over the year but how could she add or subtract when she didn't know when it had started. (The word 'conception' was one she avoided as she avoided all other words that had any relation to the sexual act.)

The child must have come! They must be somewhere. She imagined Columbine perhaps struggling in a dark corner, the baby half in and half out. The shed! Perhaps she'd run there to be private. Jessica raced downstairs and out in the back garden. But no! There were all her boxes, her tools, her workbench, the little heaps of sawdust, undisturbed exactly as she'd left them.

Back in through the house and out into the street she ran, banging doors behind her, her shoes clattering on the kitchen tiles. The street was dawn-empty. A distant beast, bullock or cow, gave a lamentable cry. There was the noise of the cistern in the house next door and then silence. She stood like a stopped pendulum, not knowing which way to run.

It must have been my hysterics that woke the neighbours. Not the deaf man, of course, but the ones on the right-hand side. She came out straggling and strealing, looking like I must look now when I'm woken early from sleep. Of course they knew why I was screaming. While we lived in our fool's paradise, imagining that only the headmistress knew, everybody in the village was exulting in my sister's pregnancy. Her pathetic anorak had hidden nothing from those sex-obsessed eyes.

I was carried or pushed into the house. I was raucous, incoherent, they—the grey faces (suddenly there were many)— were collected around me, gloating. I was shoved into bed, pills put in my mouth, a glass of water knocked against my clenched teeth. They threatened me with the doctor but it wasn't I who needed the doctor, I tried to tell them. No one seemed to care. It was as if they'd caught one fish and didn't care about the other.

But, as soon as they left, thinking me asleep, I leapt up again, crept downstairs, ran out the back and across the fields. How did I know where to go? But there was purpose in my running, that I do remember. My vision was distorted—from the pills, I expect. I ran and ran, sliding over ditches, and through a bit of plough and over a further ditch beyond Long's farm. And there she was, lying in the muck, her neck twisted, her eyes closed, a small twig tangled in her hair. There was something beyond her bared feet, dark like liver, slimy. Then I noticed its shape and a little white shining through the slime,

21

like a red apple with a bite out of it. It was the child's head. It was asleep, too, it seemed.

I bent over my sister, took her in my arms.

'My dove, my Columbine, wake up. It's me, Jessica.' I knelt beside her, cradled her and kissed her many times. Her body was limp. I lay down with her, opening my shirt to pour my own warmth into her. The long grass rode up around us, a thrush perched on a blackthorn. His song was sweet.

But that is all. If only I could creep back into that tunnel. The light is there somewhere, deep amongst the million cells of my brain. I can catch the sound of a twig cracking or a branch wheezing. Someone could have followed me, seen us together, carried us home. Perhaps it doesn't matter. Will I leave it there? Did I die then with her, to be reborn in a web for four years until finally released by *his* death to live alone for the next fifty surrounded by my boxes, my pieces of wood, my delicate filigree patterns, my chisels, my complicated machines, my meaningless carvings which have made me famous, rich. Yes I will leave us there, me holding the wall of your body, you relaxed in my arms, keeping the secret of your sleep, your child's sleep. Unable to keep the two lives going, you chose rather to leave me barren in the short death of days. Maybe we shared those days together. Yes I'll leave it there.

The Launching

NO MEAN DEHYDRATING WINE at this party. No, no! The publishers had done her proud, or rather twisted the arms of the distillers. Ice clinked in the massive glasses of vodka, gin and whiskey as plumes of smoke rose above the clamour.

She walked in carefully to disguise the fact that she was already partially drunk and perhaps also hoping to disguise her dread of the forthcoming boredom that would settle on her like a hen on its nest.

At least they were all women. A tide of women. Her publisher whispered, 'You're late.' She explained that she couldn't read her watch—a digital watch that she'd been given at a garage.

'Please read it for me and tell me how late I am.'

'The photographers, you know.'

'I am old and don't photograph well. Stevie Smith …'

The publisher drew her along into a side room: 'Please co-operate, Emily.'

'Didn't mind looking old but hated looking dead. Stevie Smith.'

'Oh Emily it's not that bad. I'm sorry it's that mean guy from the *News*. He'll be here in a sec.'

Yes, the uncouth man swished in accompanied by yet another. 'I thought you said …'

'Yes I know, pet. There was a muddle.'

'Ah Mrs …, Ms …' He looked at his notes. 'Ms Gilchrist.'

Emily gazed at the harvest head of her publisher: 'Help me.'

'Please, pet. Banks, you know. We've got to sell.'

'Yes, banks.'

Emily ran. 'Not yet,' she cried, elbowing her way to the bar, between long tables laden with multi-tiered sandwiches and canapés that the guests swept into their mouths as though they hadn't eaten for weeks. She was amazed to see so many unknown faces. She was getting out of touch. She scrabbled her skinny hand towards the barman, stating her need for a large whiskey. Her hand is covered in moles like the back of a fig. Normally she is not served in unfamiliar bars; barmen think she's a tinker and throw her out. This barman had the same unfriendly eye but he was not in a position to refuse her. Feeling a little less shaky she returned to the company.

Trapped again. The press-man herded her into a corner. 'Do you think this internal gardening will eventually change the weather?' she asked as she was pressed against trailing greenery. But he didn't smile. He shouted for Ms Mahoney. 'Now you must both hold the book and look at me.'

'Why can't we look at the book?'

'Look at me,' he said crossly. Emily knew what that meant. Another hideous photograph in the evening paper.

'Now, Ms Gilchrist, how often do you visit your native Ballyferrin?'

'Never.'

'Come, come. Your play is clearly set in your native town. There is an asylum there, is there not?'

'There is indeed. A very nasty place. My mother was dehumanised there.' She began to feel weak. She should never say anything to reporters, and here she was as usual yapping away about things that should remain under the pillow of secrecy for ever.

'So is there anything autobiographical in your play?'

She bit her lip and said 'No,' limply. He looked suspicious and made a note.

'You have children, Ms Gilchrist.'

'Eight.'

'You must be a great character.'

'No,' she replied. 'I am not a great character. The trouble with you *bastards* is that you think a woman who does anything except wait hand and foot on a man must be some sort of female Frankenstein—a character that children laugh at behind their hands. Supposing Mr…'

'Meagher,'

'Thank you, Meagher, that I was interviewing you on the golf course and you told me you were a journalist and I said you must be a great character how would you feel?' She was tearing ivy up by the roots when Ms Mahoney tried to calm her.

'Perhaps you're over-reacting.'

'I'm not overfucking-reacting. Just because I'm ordinary. I don't look pretty. My youngest child is twenty-one. I have to put up with this kind of insult. Middle-aged women are no good to man or beast. Once you're over eighty you'll have a new image and a new lease of popularity.'

She grumped her way to the bar and demanded further refreshment. The wad of anger gradually shrank away. Luckily her outburst had been only partially observed by the guests who now resumed their treasure hunt—like herself—for drunken immobility. There was nobody she wanted to talk to.

Girls advanced with little loops of flattery, retreated quietly. She stood like a statue—friendless. Perhaps she was a nasty piece of work and didn't deserve a friend, or just too ugly.

'We feel that Emily Gilchrist has broken new ground in her study of early Irish feminist behaviour. The enormity of scholarship and research,' Ms Mahoney began, 'proves that the Irish woman was once a very considerable figure in society. It is my great pleasure to launch this very fine prize-winning play.'

This was followed by an accolade from Sister Seroya from the Holy Faith Convent who said that she personally would use the play as a foremost text in her school in the Special Studies class. That it was time that Irish woman reinstated herself as a national force. That the considerable work that had been done over the last ten years by the various women's movements was estimable, but we must go forward all the time. And she stepped down amid deafening applause.

Nothing like a progressive religious to bring tears to the eyes of atheists, thought Emily gloomily as she weaved back to the bar. The barmen were pulling down ominous shutters—the magic cave was disappearing. 'Just one more,' she pleaded, but no, the accordion-pleated barrier fell before her. Utterly defeated, she wedged back through the crowd.

'Where are you going?'

She looked into the squarest blackest fringe she'd ever seen.

'To a quiet brown pub,' Emily said.

'May I come, too?'

'The pressman called me a character,' she said as they walked.

'These things…' the other added: 'I'm staying at the Shamrock.'

She was tall—over six foot—and had a broad Liverpool accent. Emily felt the bubble of fun there and something else ticked at the neck of her memory. A picture? No, not a picture. A thread from the radio, half-heard? The voice. 'I know,' she said, 'you are *the* Dr O'Flaherty, the definitive expert on the Poorhouses of Ireland.'

'And you are *the* Ms Gilchrist, winner of the Remington Historical Play Award.'

The pavement shone like frost. The marketplace shelved the day's debris—cabbage leaves, daffodils, tomatoes, oranges, onions. 'How strange and eerie it is,' she took Emily's hand.

The cobblestones expanded in the moonlight, her hand was soft against Emily's work-worn palm. They kissed under a spear of light between two folded canopies.

'I love you,' Emily said.

The following day, dusty pages caressed Emily's fingernails. The brown dome of the library was contained in a misty glow from the many reading-lamps. She had seen her to the airport and now she would be in Hull, or York, or Bath or Leeds, her strong eyes searching out the little tit-bits that had escaped notice for so many years, correlating, annotating. 'All in a day's work,' she had said.

Yes. Emily turned her gaze back to the Victorian print of the book on her desk.

Euston

AGAIN NINA STOPPED AS IF, STANDING STILL, she'd have more control over her judgement. She had always believed that Euston Station was the exclusive property of the Irish, and this new crystalline fecundity, apart from being geographically confusing, was the opposite of lonely squalor, the top rung of the emigrant's ladder before his natural descent. Not at all dramatic, in fact, functional, shiny, dirty yes, but most discomfiting.

People streamed in all directions—there was no current to ride on, no pointer to choice or oblivion, destruction or rebirth. What a fool she was to have entertained the notion yesterday evening that herein lay the mark of her identity.

But surely just a simple unheralded hullo-goodbye? A few hours to be nursed in retrospect when she returned to Dublin inevitably in four days' time. As she had simply said to her daughter, 'I'm dropping over to see Clive.'

'It's all right Mummy, I'll mind the babies.'

She started off again, balancing with difficulty amongst a new onrush of travellers, whose unseemly flight was all the more tiring in face of her own emotional bewilderment. She knew she was going in the right direction because infallibly main line terminals point one way only and this dreary knowledge brought her to the very edge of the crowd, indeed until only rolling stock and the odd African porter could be spotted in the

28

distance along the dull echoing expanse.

Was this as it had been ten, fifteen years ago? Was it as it had been when London Midland and Scottish steam engines puffed languidly in? When clerks, top-hatted, with quill pen in one hand, ink bottle in the other, set their marks on incoming and outgoing goods, a hundred years ago?

'Yes, Mummy, I'm sure I'll be all right. You go ahead and have a good time.'

One of the porters approached on his trolley; with eyes as soft as a heifer's he looked down at her, stopped his machine, lapped his hands, the one over the other, drawled slowly, 'You looking for something, Miss?'

'Yes, I … There used to be a fellow worked this side of the station. Name of Clive. He, I think, was known as Harry to his fellow workers.'

'Harry. Oh I know him. He still works here. He been here only half an hour ago.'

'Where is his office?' Little beads of fear ran down her back.

'You come, I show you.' And she followed the porter to a solitary office marked INWARD FISH.

Nina knocked. 'Do you think it's his tea break?'

'Harry take tea breaks, sometimes dey like lunch breaks,' the dark face broke up like a torn negative; the bass laugh echoed against the hollow roar of the loudspeaker which called out platforms, times, destinations.

She knocked again. 'Are you likely to see him when he comes back?'

'Best thing you,' the slow drawl lingered, 'go up to the tea bar nearest platform 1. I tell Harry you there. OK?'

She dragged her suitcase once more the long leaden length.

E.U.S.T.O.N.

No haven for the brown fibre suitcase, baggy trousers— arse down to the knees.

EUSTON.

Did the dole queues in Camden Town still begin here? And like Bartleby the Scrivener, had Clive not outlasted time?

In the tea bar she lagged with her plastic tray. She handed out her thirty pence and took it to the Formica table round which people, like bundles of clothing sat in positions of anticipation. Period of waiting per paper cup equals infinity.

Her nearest neighbour sighed like a horse. Would she learn patience from her? From that pale stoical Asiatic face?

Whenever order is disturbed, whenever disorder rises, I create myself anew, she whispered. Would her first rise of joy as she stepped off the train revitalise her now? At least she wasn't in Dublin! She could walk in and out of this tea bar a hundred times and no one would stop her. They might rob her or mug her but they wouldn't ask her where she was going.

The Indian lady's clothes stirred like rain. Was she longing for the hot streets of Madras or Bombay or did she still respond to the magic of London? Nina wanted to cry out to her their special fortune for being able to share the magnetic powers of this great metropolis, but how?

Just supposing she told her she was running away from a mad husband who beat her every day? That she was over here to re-establish some long discarded identity? Would she move away, pull her eastern saris more tightly round her wool-clad arms? Would she call the attendant?

What had she left behind? The changing seasons of St Stephen's Green, the blossom from the May trees in other people's gardens? The petals shed amongst the plastic bags on the banks of the Grand Canal, the cherry trees, fuchsia bushes, lilac, nodding just out of reach in Fitzwilliam Square? If she mentioned these things would she stir in the heart of this lady the memory of the sluggish current on the brown waters of the Chambal or the Narbada, the scent of spices in the markets, or just old sores, the self-abasement of hunger, the penance of the underdog in some unspeakable slum?

But Nina, sitting back, allowed excitement to invade her. Was not the present trustworthy? She must not think. Not of home. Had not the boat and train journey nearly done for her? The political chatter at the next table had insinuated into her consciousness, had kept her on edge, stricken for having left her daughter in charge at home.

But oh God! She stared with eyes of glass at her surroundings. What had she done?

Or was she getting delirious from lack of sleep? What about the baby? The elder boy had that habit of putting an unsterilised bottle in the baby's mouth. The baby might get gastroenteritis!

Jesus!

Unwittingly she hit the Indian lady with her elbow.

'Sorry! Terribly!' She gathered pieces of sugar paper, cigarette butts and dirty plastic spoons and put them in the ashtray.

'It's all right,' the lady said with another wide sigh.

'Are you waiting for a train?'

'My son. He come. He come ten o'clock from Manchester.'

Nina looked at her; the digital clock said eleven forty-nine. She watched the five and nought settle into place.

'Do you think he missed the train?'

'Could be.'

'Did you see the train come in?' Nina pursued.

'Yes. I see it,'

'When's the next one?'

'It come twelve.'

'Ah,' Nina said, relaxing. 'You haven't long to wait now.'

'He come twelve,' the lady said, satisfied.

They fell back on silence. The changing area of Nina's

consciousness was attacked once more. The middle one! Her three-year-old daughter, sweet love, had complained of a pain last night. Just when she was leaving. Appendicitis! If Charlotte hadn't already rushed her to hospital it would turn into peritonitis! She saw the sulphurous liquid seeping into the peritoneum leaving its deathly trail. She groaned so loudly the Indian lady fixed her eyes on her. No, no. How stupid! The whole world, it seemed, was shaking her around like a single pea. She searched for new words to tell the Indian lady, but she had retreated into a dismissive shell. An old man had settled down opposite and was devouring a sausage roll. After each mouthful he brought out from his overcoat pocket a stained handkerchief with which he dabbed his mouth between each bite. No small waves of recognition there. How could she tell him that her little girl lay in her cot, her sweet small head turning this way and that, unaware … unaware … Her short life unrocked, her mother gallivanting in London!

She jumped up. The Indian woman too was leaving. Surely, coming from such an undernourished part of the world she must know about peritonitis? God knew how many children she'd buried—but through no fault of her own. Only *she* was capable of such neglect.

They banged through the glass doors. 'Madam!' but the lady was gone on ahead, edging through a circle of foreign students with packs on their backs like harvest sheaves. Nina cried again, but her voice was drowned by the loudspeaker: *Train from Manchester arriving on Platform Four.*

So she ran. *Excusez moi… Verstehen Sie?* She hurried towards the line of telephone boxes. Soundless conversation. Three boxes out of order. Independently impatient but outwardly calm, the citizens of London wait. One city man zips and unzips his briefcase. London is too large. Full of banal people making banal conversations.

IF YOU SEE AN UNATTENDED PACKAGE DO NOT TOUCH IT. NOTIFY THE STATION AUTHORITIES AT ONCE.

DO NOT PANIC.

Don't panic! A few minutes here or there!

Supposing the doctor has a hangover? It will be about twelve-thirty by the time Charlotte gets to the hospital. Quarter to one. The doctor will be edgy. Better wait till two, perhaps, if the pain isn't too bad. No, they probably have lunch shifts. But they don't often. Usually have to wait indefinitely in the out-patients. Still it might be better if she took her straight away. She'd be the first in the queue after lunch! This was crazy. A far better idea would be for her to fly home at once.

Nina hadn't seen one Irish face since her arrival. But now she searched and found—what must be—a countrywoman, probably from Tipperary.

'Excuse me, do you happen to know the price of a single fare to Dublin by plane?'

'Please?'

Another man, alone, apart; a young man with eyes the colour of hard Meath stone could be … must be … 'Excuse me …' Nina tapped his arm. Brown eyelids folded over high cheek-bones and then slowly opened, revealing the fierce pain of survival. 'So sorry … I thought …'

And if a bomb went off before she got through!

She pushed in front of a German, whose cynical bowing told a tale more terrifying, but she defied and pressed into the booth.

She dialled and a voice said 'Operator!'

God! The English are so efficient.

And that antiquated oil stove! That was likely to flare up and burn the flat down!

'Hullo!' The pained tones of her neighbour in Dublin.

'This is Missus from next door. I would be grateful if you'd get Charlotte for me?'

33

And the silence of the dropped receiver! She could see it lying on the scabby oil cloth while her neighbour slowly negotiated the basement steps; time and space means nothing to her! 'Hullo,' she said into the void in case the operator thought she was finished and cut her off.

'Hullo!' It was as if the soprano of Charlotte's voice was in the booth beside her.

'Hullo, Mummy here.'

'Mummy? Are you all right?'

'I'm fine. How's everything?'

'OK.'

'What about Jessy?'

'What about her?'

'How's her pain?'

'I don't know.'

'Did she complain of a pain this morning?'

'No.'

'How are the others?'

'OK. They've gone to the Green with Maria.'

'Is Maria there?'

'Yes.'

'Good. She'll give you a hand.'

'Yes.'

'Will you be able to manage all right?'

'Yes. Why are you ringing?'

Bleep, bleep, bleep.

'Goodbye!' Charlotte's voice, faint.

'See you in a few days.' The line was dead.

Nina looked vacantly at the sturdy machine, the twopenny, the tenpenny slots. Vanquished, she leant against the zigzag door. Nothing was solved. Her home was still at risk.

And Clive! Clive will have looked in the tea bar and gone away. Puzzled. She hadn't told the porter her name. But she couldn't stand here indefinitely. She should ring back, check on the things she had forgotten—the oil fire, the sterilised bottles, all the small things a child of fourteen would overlook. But Pascal, after all, was there too. In between his conquests and his wanderings. Was she not being unreasonably stubborn? A mother should be allowed a holiday. A holiday! She had managed well enough without one for ten years! She should have continued to do so in her martyrdom!

She left the box and drifted back to the tea bar, purchased another cup, sat at another table, waited. She was compelled to watch the door. For why not? But why? She had wasted too much time. Too many long years. Like the Indian lady.

And there she was! Yes for sure! She was coming towards her, generously. Nina half rose and the lady sat and sighed once more.

'Your son?' Nina softly said.

'Ah ha!'

'He'll surely come on the next?'

'At one-thirty!' She screwed up her face.

'Does he work in Manchester?'

'My son?' The lady's look was playful. 'He have worked. He come to see me very often!'

'He must be a good boy.'

'He not good.'

'Oh. But he's good to come and see you often. Lots of children never bother about their parents at all. Just go their own way. Let their parents starve. Yes, he must care about you.'

'He not good,' the lady repeated.

Did this patient humour represent the weariness of ancient Indian culture? The lady's movements were all slow as if she would go on moving for so long until one day, without a word of complaint, she would move no more. Then, presumably, her bad son would have her buried as cheaply as possible.

'His father was a good man,' the lady went on.

'You have just the one son?'

'I have two sons and one daughter.'

'I have two sons and two daughters,' Nina said.

'They babies?'

'They … mostly babies.'

'Who look after them?'

'Well … the neighbours. The neighbours are minding them for a week.'

'You have good neighbours,' the lady stated.

'Wonderful. They're in Dublin.'

'Dublin!' the lady said as if she had said Bangladesh. 'It very uncomfortable in Dublin. You have much troubles.'

'Yes. What part of London do you live in?' Now the lady knew. Knew she had abandoned them. Abandoned them in a city, the lady thought, that was in the centre of a war. She hurried on. 'I know London. I used to live here.' Nina could not breathe.

'I live in Chalk Farm.'

'Oh good, that's a nice area.' A small sob, like a dropped stitch held.

'It not nice.'

'Well. I suppose there are some pretty rough parts of Chalk Farm. It depends on what part you live in.'

'I near the tube.'

'It's not so nice near the tube.'

And no interest in her woes or guilts.

'And anyway,' she went dully on, 'your son. He'll stay there with you when he arrives.'

'He stay.'

There was no wisdom here. Cynical, yes. But wise, no.

Supposing she had told her the whole truth? That she lived with a bastard who beat her every day, who often left her for weeks at a time without money while he floosied around with other women. Would she simply have shrugged her shoulders

36

saying 'you brought it on yourself', or would she have offered sympathy, advice? Nina didn't care any more. She got up realising the futility of it all.

'I'm going,' she shouted rudely. 'Going to find a friend. Someone who loves me!'

The lady laughed unpleasantly. 'You no find!' she said.

Blinded by rage, Nina rushed from the table. A wave of people fell in like shale. Caught in the doorway, she was tangled, shoved, released, she lost impetus, wandered, bumped blindly, tripped, longed to lie down on one of the benches and close her eyes till the time came for the train back to Liverpool. Then she could pretend. Pretend she had never come. Never had hope in her heart.

But she did stray. She strayed towards the end platform whose blind lugubrious offices bordered Eversholt Street. Had she written, warned Clive, then the protest of her guilt would not have assailed her. They used to talk of their revolutionary discipline. Where was her revolutionary discipline now? Everything in her was insipid since she had married Pascal. Her music forgotten. For there had been music once, she did think.

She saw West Indian women attacking a train with wide brooms and dustpans. They shrieked at each other as if they were in a high wind. They, too, would mock if they knew. As she passed within earshot she heard one of them say, 'My, oh my.'

The door was still closed. There was a complex picture of this man behind the door. And time, she must allow, to redirect her impulses. On her upended suitcase she sat then, unrolled the centuries behind her. She saw his large blunt-fingered hands holding the plough in the Constable canvas, the triangular bony face watching the Wye flooding, the long arm lying on the rump of the big shire horse. She saw his son and his son's son turning his back on the hymn of England's

37

countryside and grabbing some obscure knowledge from the grime of the industrial midlands, and he, this man-behind-the-door, the progenitor of that hardy body of men—English, Irish, Scottish—who had worked to make England a once powerful industrial force. And what of now? What of Nina? Fingers of light pointed down from the high glass dome above. The ebb and flow of her moods had emptied her out like a bucket. She had censored her reasons for journeying to this spot so harshly that she could do nothing now, only sit on listlessly, bent elbows on knees, biting the collar of her jacket till it was chewed limp, till, in fact, a new commotion started up—a goods train had snaked quietly in and the clamour and vibrations attacked her on all sides. Voices cautioned. She was in the way.

'Sorry!'

The unfulfilment of her journey was her last insidious weapon.

The perspective of the platform, Clive's office, the goods train itself, receded behind her. She did not look back.

'Mummy!' Charlotte came running out of the back room. 'Why are you back so soon? Did you see my father? What did he say? Did you show him my photograph?' The child laid the questions one on top of the other like pages of a book. Her voice reached her as if she were in another element. As though she, Nina, were under water and she couldn't breathe or break the seal of her silence.

Outside it was raining; transparent lozenges squeezed through the ill-fitting window frame and ran down the inside wall. Her youngest son stood in the middle of the floor holding up his rubber pants with one hand and his piece of blanket in the other.

'But Mummy!'

Nina picked up the baby and pressed her wet nose into the back of his neck, young flesh against lips like India rubber.

The words came, then, pulpy and unattached. 'Has Pascal been around?'

'No.'

'Good.' She put the baby back on the floor and went to the sink and began to wash the dishes that were piled up in cold greasy water.

Night Rider

1. THE NIGHTS

THE POOLS OF MUD WERE THE HOOF MARKS; each step was a careful putting down of the heavy boot and a removal of the boot so that the noise would not sound in the yard, would not disturb the sleeping couple in the house with walls shaded purple, beyond the yard walls, the walls made purple by the light of a reassuring moon. Beyond these pools of mud, these hoof marks, was the line of chestnut trees. The trees were skinned of their leaves, but the slant drained down and last autumn's leaves made an avenue of soft mould. Patrick Gallagher had left the old bike beyond the back gate which was really an oak door, the gate that let into Cathcart's yard; he had left it leaning against the powdery walls where the dried up concrete dusted off with the brush of the handlebars. Cathcart father and daughter! Those kind sleep comfortably! Patrick ambled on in his half-wit fashion, his thoughts flying ahead of him like birds, summer swallows that skimmed the ground before rain. He quickened his pace and passed from the mud into the avenue of mould that fell in swathes between the high roots that spread along the ground; greasy chestnut roots. His sloppy figure rose and fell as the moonlight pierced its way between the bare branches, as it made the field below spread out like dough till it came together at the bottom of the hill in a cluster of blackthorn that covered the old well. The bushes were fenced off in case the brood mares would stumble and shy away with bruised fetlocks from the stony ground. He didn't look down the hill, now, nor up into the sky either, but ploughed on towards the heavy gate far beyond that and the stables with the horses, the mares asleep there with their deep sloping backs, their narrow heads, long silk manes and heavy tails that shuddered like the waves on the February lake beyond the convent where he spent his days, his nights.

As yet he didn't know how he'd get through the gate; as yet he didn't know *if* he would get through, but he would be sly if it was locked; he'd get the better of it somehow. There was a handle latch on the door; he could see it now beyond the sheet of light between the trees and the wall; the light warned him that eyes might see him if he went up on it. He stood then in the last of the shade, his overweight body a blur against the headlands, his gaze on the steel latch. Would it lift? Would there be a bolt on the inside? All these kinds of things he had seen in his long blameless life; a life from which all blame had been removed because of the queer brain he had. He had lived in a box for a long time until he had ambled off to the mill, the ruin of a mill up at Confey where he had spluttered without words until the nuns had come and he had been driven in a car. The spontaneous jerks of his limbs had jolted against the front seat of the vehicle and he had tried to still them with his hands in case they would send him back into the box. The nun had said, 'God love him.' Then gradually the limbs had stopped gyrating; there were others in the convent worse than he was; others that couldn't lift the hands to the face that had to be fed; who grunted and ran with rivulets of water all day while the nuns wiped them down. Yes, he had learned to control his legs, had learnt to talk in a slow manner, had learnt to lean against the nun for a smile and helped to make the beds with little gay jumps each time she sent the sheet flying across the room and he'd catch it and tuck it in like an envelope. And then some of the other children had disappeared and he'd stayed on in the passing years to hoe the lawn and the avenue and trundle after the gardener till the old barrow was full up with weeds and small pebbles. 'You'll have it all dug away,' the gardener said. And then Patrick had got on the bike and when the wobbling stopped he knew he was the same as many people. 'As good as the best of them,' the nun said. So they sent him into the town for the messages and when he stood in Hogan's supermarket he'd try to get near the girl at the cash desk for the smile. 'He's a harmless eejit,' she said.

The nun told him to take a spin every Thursday afternoon and they gave him a few shillings for himself and an old homburg for his head as his hair had begun to bald, although he was not yet turned thirty. As the weeks went by and each Thursday he'd pedalled the roads, he'd taken to following the young lady from Cathcart's stud, Miss Cathcart, as she'd ridden out the big horse, he just the few paces behind and always watchful in case she'd take a dart of a glance at him and give him a skelp. The long grasses at the edge of the camber of the side road leading up to Cathcarts made a good bed for the crazy Patrick and there he'd idle in the summer, the homburg well down on the flat skull and the round face grained with a cleavage of dust at each side of the rose-bud mouth and when she'd pass he'd hump the bike on to the tarmac and shove along behind her.

Every Thursday then made him feel this ease inside him, an ease that had left him and he had not known since his body had grown into a kind of man's and the nun had said that he was too old to be making beds and the square of lawn had been given over to him. There was nothing there to give him ease; in summer the red rhododendrons would shed petals and Patrick would stare beyond the bushes for hours at a time as if to part the leaves with his gaze and see something that was not there;

that he couldn't explain. Once he said the word 'love' and the handles of the barrow lifted in his patty hands and the barrow keeled over on its side; and then he was down on his knees scooping the weeds and pebbles and righting the barrow; had said the word again, his round mouth leaking water. He had run from the word, pushing the heavy barrow in front of him, searching over his shoulder as he went to see had they heard him and feeling an ache in his back as though the box in which he had lain as a child would push against his spine as it had once done.

But now, the deadness of his life forgotten, he was still standing in the shelter of the trees dreading the open space between him and the door, but the strength of his desire to be with the horse, to be like the young one, or to be her, began to loosen his limbs and with a faltering plunge he crossed the strip of moonlight and fell with his shoulder against the door; he swung out of the metal hasp and thumbed it down and the door opened inwards.

Although he had watched Miss Cathcart dismount to open this door, although he had lurked over the road well above the line of chestnuts, he had never in his life seen the interior of this yard. The very idea had never entered his head till the night before when suddenly, on the brink of sleep, the notion had come to him to enter this yard, lead out the big horse, relying on the February moon with its soft light to guide him, when he knew that father and daughter would be in bed. But now, when his plan was almost completed, the huge space before him, the snowy cobbles, the line of stables, caused his thoughts to scatter, he felt overcome with that sullenness that often lay on him for days, that heavy stupidity that made each footstep pain, each effort of lifting the barrow, gathering the mosses and raking the gravel something he had to lunge at, that took his body out of control and established in the minds of those who noticed him that beyond making minor habit-formed movements his bodily impulses would never stray.

Yet in some way the choice of action in this blank yard no longer seemed to belong to him. The brightly painted stable doors, red by day, were black, forbidding in the starch of light. He swung back the door of the centre stable and looked into the box. The big horse that Miss Cathcart rode out every day arched its neck and stretched its back at the sudden intrusion, but as Patrick opened the bottom half of the door and stumbled in the horse pricked its ears forward and let a light whinny run through its nostrils as at the approach of a friend—a mare perhaps or the stable boy who fed him at seven every morning. Patrick, oblivious, took the head-collar that hung from a hook above the door and went to the horse's head as the animal bent down obligingly and allowed the crazy one to slip it over its ears.

Excited by the warmth of the silken neck, Patrick ran his cheek along it as he led the animal into the yard. There the horse stood high above him, no trace of fear, no ripples of apprehension ran over his body, no harm between them; Patrick's innocence established unbreakable trust between man and beast.

He must go into the field, he knew, away from the windows that watched the yard, somewhere where a rock or a stump might help him climb onto the animal's back. And in the hill field at last he did find a stump, and in spite of his wide jacket managed to scramble on and hold fast with his thighs, the rope from the head collar grasped with one hand, the mane with the other, and the animal's heat between his legs. He eased the horse down the field, caressing its sides with his heels as he had seen the young one do. His mind was full now; little whistling noises came through his nose as the animal walked along with its high stride; his weak intelligence no longer seemed his enemy.

Patrick had never known anything before, he felt,

compared with what he knew now. That he could feel secure so high above the ground, that he could move forward and share the squat shadow that followed them while the moon raced across the sky behind lacy clouds and stayed in the one spot all the time. He knew that he could be the same each night he came here while the moon was asserting her powers over him. In some strange way he was conscious of this.

And so he was. For six nights his body followed the same pattern and the horse who appeared to expect him now would raise its head and whinny even while his feet crept over the cobbles and the light whinny would ripple over the yard, striking apprehension into Patrick in case the watchful windows lit up and he was seen to enter the stable.

But all went well until the seventh night when a blanket covered the waning moon and, trusting the presence of his courage, his madness protecting him from fear, Patrick mounted as usual in the field. But he felt immediately that something was different; not as on other nights. The previous night he had heard a noise and, sliding from the animal, had left it to graze as he zig-zagged up the hill to climb the wall and mount his bike. Now it was different; the big house in the darkness had sprung into life. Lights flashed on in every window it seemed, voices cracked like shot in the frosty air. With a moan he fell from the animal and all around were the faces he dreaded.

II THE TRIAL

Jim Cathcart came into the county court with his daughter Deborah. He entered circumspectly, his daughter's hopeful look an irritation he was trying to subdue. He sat apart from the others, the high collar of his overcoat shielding his narrow bleached face. Deborah, equally irritated by her father, shrugged into the crowd searching for her friend Olivia Plunkett whom she saw now chin deep in furs, huddled on the third bench from the back of the courthouse.

This strategic point had been chosen by Olivia so that as soon as Deborah's case was heard she might quietly leave by the side door; both puzzled and intrigued by the strange happenings at the stud, she was bored now and even agreed with Deborah's father that the matter should have been dropped. Taking action against the village idiot (for that is how she thought of Patrick Gallagher) seemed to her futile, almost ugly. However, she was loyal to Deborah and for this reason would sit it out.

Jim hoped neither to recognise nor be recognised by any of his neighbours. His famous stud was about to be the butt end of a joke in the local press. Publicity of any kind was abhorrent to him. But the others were getting restless from the wait and all craned when at last a nun entered trying to drag Patrick after her. She was having difficulties getting him through the door and when her soothing failed she began to panic. She looked round and round, her pert eyes pleading, but the crowd remained virtuously intact, watching Gallagher hang-dog in the doorway until the sergeant gave him a push from behind and he half fell in. Small whistles of fear issued from the red-ring mouth and his sloppy actions and retarded look made people gasp with anticipation. His eyes were almost invisible, buried in his swollen cheeks, the pigment of his skin darkened by fear. Deborah and Olivia turned, too, and watched the nun squashing him into a seat, the morbid agencies in their blood exacerbated by his nearness; they murmured to each other, laughed.

No sign of the judge. Jim's watch said 11.15. Deborah, always twisting, began to feel other influences—her father's unease, Olivia's boredom, the waning curiosity of the people on either side whom the winter village had driven in, either to answer or question or simply to observe—and for the first time she questioned her motives in taking action against Gallagher. Were her need to score over her father, her own exhibitionism and her desire to be the centre of attention the real reasons she was pressing on with the case? She tried to reassure herself that she had others; she genuinely cared about the horses, liked to run things efficiently and see that the stud farm remained a viable enterprise. She combed her fingers through her short Saxon hair and watched the flowing in of the last few stragglers. There was the inevitable Declan Piggott, local solicitor, with his inevitable charges, this time two teenagers, undernourished strays, breakers and enterers into places forbidden, dreaming of caves of acquisition that would bring eternal freedom. The solicitor also looked diminished, the squander of the previous night on his brow. His clothes even showed a certain indistinction; the pile of his coat was unbrushed and a stiff line of dandruff stuck to his collar. They, too, found a seat and subsided. The last in was a small painted girl, starry eye shadow, cinnamon cheeks, half grown in a stony world. Her high plastic heels made a bright clatter as she edged along and found a place beyond the teenagers.

Olivia was conscious of her companion's optimism but unaware of her misgivings. Like a boat moored offshore she wanted to be gone. She had spent the previous night drinking with the judge and had woken in the blue morning and remembered with horror that she had promised Deborah that she'd attend the court. She had floundered from her comfortable bed into an atmosphere of chaos that seemed to cling to her lately in spite of her efforts to control her life. Yes, her life was straying out on all sides; drink and the weight of middle age were taking over. She rose now, murmured to Deborah and eased her way along the benches, reaching the antechamber just as the bile entered her mouth. In desperation she lit a cigarette, knowing it would only make her feel worse. Exhaling, she made the sergeant cough; he was dead sick of the long wait, too, and the nearness of Olivia did not improve his temper.

At the sound of a car Olivia trod on the half-smoked butt and went back to rejoin her friend.

Judge McSharry came in carrying a briefcase and a sheaf of papers. He settled himself on the podium like a frog on a raft and gazed over his glasses at the assemblage. Long-sightedness had caused a deep furrow between his brows and the frown was accentuated this morning by a fierce hangover. Working on the circuit led to long sessions drinking in country hotels. He caught sight of Olivia. He recalled the sophisticated malice with which she had cornered him the previous night and how their mutual drinking had hit them like a tumult. They had amused each other mightily. He knew he liked her in spite of everything going against her, her size, and her ultimate awful loneliness. Why did he attract these huge women? Every county in Ireland seemed to produce one of these lumpy unattractive dispossessed females. He allowed himself a slight chuckle.

Patrick Gallagher, squashed beside the nun, was cowed into apathy. He strained to understand the words of the solicitor whose inaudible voice buzzed away in the distance while case after case was dealt with. One small thought he clung to—the memory of the two shots that had crashed through the frosty air and turned his life into a concentrated circle of terror. He craved release from the mystery of insanity and the inability to grasp reason. Why had the young one fired at him? He had run the wrong way, blundered, fallen in the tufted grass. He remembered also the smell of his own soiled pants as the man, the father, had been gentle, had bent over him, helped him to his feet, told him that he had done no harm. What harm was in it, anyway? Yet Patrick believed now, because the nuns told him, that he shouldn't have done it, but he didn't know why. Yes, he had done wrong and that was that. Sitting astride the big horse, making friends with it, letting it wander at will to feel ease in that way, comfort, he now knew was wrong and he would be punished. Not as he was punished always by his weak mind, but by something far worse; perhaps they would put him back in the box or tether him to a stake like the convent goat. He kept remembering how the young one had shouted something awful and how they had dragged him to the house, how the guard had come and how the young one had put the gun on the shiny oval table and how the father had removed it and put it on the floor.

'Miss Deborah Cathcart!'

Deborah rose; her fiery face gave the judge a momentary pang; she looked excitable—cruel.

On the other side of the court Garda Flynn also rose. He gave evidence that on the night of the 25th February at 2 a.m. he had been called to the house of the Cathcarts by the young lady in person. On presenting himself at that abode he had seen the accused …

'Yes, yes,' the judge said. 'What had taken place?'

Garda Flynn continued: Miss Cathcart told him she had surprised the accused riding her horse in the hill field. She told him she wished to charge the accused with the riding of the horse that night and on the previous night without her permission.

'Did you,' said the judge, turning to Deborah, 'find anything missing?'

'Well no,' Deborah said. It was simply the fact that the horse was very valuable and she was afraid it would come to harm.

'Was the animal in foal?' the judge asked, having been primed in advance that the Cathcarts owned one of the most famous studs in the county.

'It was a horse, not a mare,' Deborah replied scathingly. There was a ripple of laughter that the judge rebuked sternly.

Deborah went on to mention that previous to the night

49

in question the horse had been found in 'an awful state' roaming the grounds without its sheet.

The judge then asked what she meant by 'an awful state'.

'Well, it was muddy,' she said. 'It could have caught a chill from having been out all night. Furthermore,' she insisted, 'the animal is highly strung and could have been badly unsettled for life.'

'Was it upset?' the judge snapped.

'Strangely, no.'

'Is the accused fit to plead?'

The nun rose and stated that she didn't think Patrick should stand. She would answer for his character. He worked in the convent and although slow he was willing and obedient.

'I'm not talking about his character,' the judge rasped out.

Surprisingly Patrick ambled forward.

'That's her! The young one with the gun. She wants to shoot me.'

A murmur went round the room like the tide dragging at shingle. The judge banged his desk.

He felt his hangover returning; the long patient road of judging and being judged. His headache, the one that had woken him up in his narrow hotel bedroom …

Where am I? he wanted to say. *Am I here to despatch good and bad? I'm an old fool. I never rise beyond the level of certain impressions, not even in my dreams. I am simply waiting for the brain haemorrhage to come at me and carry me away. And then I'll lie on in one of those narrow bedrooms and the breakfast tray will be on the floor beside me. The egg will congeal, the rasher stiffen, the cold toast, the tepid tea, the softening cornflakes will bear silent witness. I will die in those nauseous waters between waking and dreaming. Dust will gather on the milk.*

'Do you admit to the charges?' he asked Patrick.

Patrick's mouth swelled with saliva.

'You broke and entered the yard of Mr and Miss Cathcart

on February 25th and'—he consulted his notes—'on six previous nights, and taking Miss Cathcart's horse from the stable did mount and ride him round the field. Why did you choose these particular nights?' The judge pulled himself up. This last question was irrelevant.

'Because there was a moon,' Patrick's voice cleared suddenly.

'But the night I found you …' Deborah interrupted.

'Address the judge.'

'The night I found him, sir, was cloudy. There was no moon.

'It was in the sky!' Patrick spat.

The judge had no feeling of life now. The flow of moral concepts had been cut off. He shouldn't have allowed the poor retarded creature to stand. Was not Gallagher better off than he? His mutterings came up from the well of the court. His talk of the moon. 'Behind the clouds in her basin.' *Man without preconceived notions is in a state of grace,* the judge unexpectedly thought.

And Gallagher kept on:

'I could have been like her if she'd let me. Her with the gun. Me and the horse was friends. Good friends.'

'Yes, yes.' The judge, too, muttered, continued: 'The purpose of these excursions?'

'I wanted to ride the big horse.'

He wanted to ride the big horse! Why pursue it? Happiness. What was that word? He hadn't thought of that word for decades. He focused on Patrick, who still muttered incomprehensible phrases. No. Comprehensible. It was easy to understand him. But why expect Gallagher to understand the rest of them? Why the hell should he? The judge was angry at last. He barked out: 'Miss Cathcart, did anyone witness the accused riding in the field?'

'My father saw him after he'd fallen from the horse.'

51

Jim Cathcart lifted his head. All this time Jim had looked at no one. He had let the interchanges sow their small seeds of anguish in his heart. His thoughts had channelled back through time. His wife's death, her hospitalisation, her plea to be allowed home, his refusal in the hope that some way she might recover. Her money that he had used to set up his stud farm. That fruitful time after Deborah was born and how they used to kiss the baby so much he could still feel the bounce of flesh, soft young flesh on his lips. Then when his wife had died his sensibility had been given such a jolt that all feeling seemed to have left him. He used to wander among the brood mares absentmindedly; a woman had been employed to take care of his daughter. He had accumulated money. The stud had flourished. Inheriting his eye for valuable horseflesh, his daughter growing up had virtually taken over the business.

'So that is why Deborah carries a gun and kicks the simple-minded ...' Unknown to each other Jim's thoughts began to run along the same lines as the judge's. When the latter asked him did he think there was a danger of Gallagher's returning to trouble them, he answered shortly: 'No.'

The judge bent over and asked the nun, Sister Mary Agnes, if she would answer for her charge and see that he didn't leave the convent after dark in future.

'Oh, yes, sir.'

Judge McSharry thought it was queer how his headache came and went. He pictured a small clot forming on one of the millions of blood vessels that fed his brain cells. But he still wanted to animate Gallagher, to invest him with the abilities of the average human being who makes the decisions that guide the lines of his life; to put tensions in the ageless face that would show he had expanded the ideas that were born in him, so that he would fall in with the idiotic set of values society imposed. Jim Cathcart had somehow let him down, he felt, angry again. He had been startled by the intuition that had livened Jim's face momentarily and then dropped from him when the inevitable shutter came down. Was he, Gabriel McSharry, going mad now after all these tedious years of carved sanity? He felt an urgent need to give the poor demented half-wit a story to tell. Everyone should have a story. The judge thought of the story of his own life—some sixty years of thwarted ambitions— and wondered if the terrible vague isolation of Gallagher's life would now be better or worse for its seven days risk than the sum of his own days which, when divided into parts, presented an entire life without distinction. Five times that morning he had given the probation act to criminals of varying degrees and he recalled how often he had made speeches about gangsters roaming the roads and hammered sentences on them, keeping his own virtue untarnished. What sort of an old mumbler was he? He stole a look at Miss Cathcart—the sheen of health that she projected from her sturdy body made him shudder again: if he'd been in Gallagher's socks he'd have taken a jump at her instead of risking his life on a mad horse in the middle of the night. Judge McSharry laughed, hoarse, ugly. Everyone shifted—a few laughed too—like children giggling in church.

'Probation act!'

Jim Cathcart sighed. The crowd, unstiffening from the endless morning, blew on their fingers and hurried toward the exit. Jim let them disappear before following. He did not want to talk then or perhaps ever again. He wanted a slow diminution of his life. He would secretly always acknowledge his daughter's beauty while knowing he was the cause of the unbridgeable gap between them. He would admire her ultimate practicality, her many talents, but they would never, never touch. He had stopped kissing her one day; incredibly so. Other men fondled her now and he knew them not. Doors opened and closed sometimes during the long nights—that was all. Fatigued, he went out into the sharp sunlight. He realised, too, now, that intention was a product of circumstance. He noticed

53

in passing that Patrick Gallagher and the nun were still in the antechamber. He did not look at them, nor did he care to look at his daughter who was climbing into her Triumph Spitfire with Olivia Plunkett. He went straight home.

The nun tried to persuade Patrick to move. But just as entering the courthouse, the leaving of it made him brute obstinate. He had stuck his hat on his head and the patchy cheeks and frightened eyes were hidden under the brim.

'You're free,' the nun said, presuming he hadn't understood what had happened. Before this, nobody had known what went on in Patrick Gallagher's mind. Nobody had cared. They presumed that his catatonic condition was the outcome of some brain damage or congenital illness. For many years he had inhabited that old barracks of a mill, had made his bed in one of the empty rooms and distressing evidence of this animal lair had kept most people as far away as possible. As time went on, however, the village had developed a certain guilt about him, and in particular the nuns, who had decided to take him in. In due course it was found that he was not without the use of certain faculties; had he not managed unaided for years? He had been given menial tasks, an old shed was converted as living quarters, and although slow and sloppy he stayed on in the convent 'paying his way' and was soon forgotten as the half-crazed idiot who had frightened small children and caused well-heeled citizens to turn away. Sister Agnes wondered, now, how they would keep watch of him at night. She knew he was harmless but he had managed to make trouble; she was wearied of it.

She dragged him out into the flinty air; the northeast wind blew through her clothing and he, too, looked perished. Come on, now, she begged, backing hopefully in the direction of the convent road till he pulled out of his stupor and began ambling after her. It was a good mile and a half from the village, walking one after the other, sometimes she leading, and when shoved up on the grass verge by a passing truck he would shuffle on ahead, and in this way finally they reached the convent gates.

The convent seemed to have been designed by an architectural schizophrenic. Styles old and new divorced from aesthetics had expanded the building right down to the road, and at the sight of these concrete lumps Patrick stopped again. Some fundamental urge reawoke in him, the same urge, perhaps, that had made him suddenly rise from his bed in the middle of the night and go to Cathcart's yard. The tingling of his blood when he'd mounted the big horse in the field.

The nun grabbed at him but he pulled away. His fears began to inhabit her; she left him and ran up the avenue shouting for help. He stood there, reliving that last night and how it had come about. How action had converted action into energy and he had ridden out the big horse night after night; how he had bumped along on the animal's back, keeping balance by the weight of his heavy boots which dangled on either side and how the animal had reacted—yes—to his innocence as animals will, strolling along and stopping occasionally to grab small tufts of grass which pushed up beneath the surface of the frost-hard ground. And the swishing of the animal's hooves had been the only sound for miles. And then he remembered how the moon had gone behind the blanket of cloud and the big house had lit up and the trees beyond had thrown out unearthly shapes, the bushes had moved, the shadows had broken and reformed, shots had been fired, and he had fallen and run and stumbled and run.

And he was running now. Without realising it he had crossed the road into Herr Rosenstein's farm. There was a small wasted patch of field in front of a large dyke that the German had cut to border his property. Patrick ran along the edge of the dyke. This time he knew he must fall before the shots came; the distant screams had begun. But his shoes clogged up with clay. In a gulch one minute, on hard ground the next, he finally fell into a wedge of earth and was trapped. Apathy entered him, wrapped him up, held him down. No man or woman would drag him from it now; his short legs jerked as he let the March water enter his open mouth, his eyes, his nostrils. Patrick was, as before, an extinct creature caught in a lock of time.

Deborah Cathcart entered the breakfast room. She picked up the local paper that was folded by her plate. She smiled at the excellent photograph of herself and Olivia climbing into her car. She would buy the original and frame it.

Jim Cathcart came in. He wore his bedroom slippers but otherwise he was dressed in his normal checked jacket and narrow Terylene trousers; They've got it all in!'

Jim pulled his chair back and sat down.

'The whole story. And look. Apparently he tried to run away but they caught him and he's been locked up in hospital. Isn't that lucky?'

Jim took the enamel lid off his bacon and eggs. He peered at his breakfast tray for some time and then replaced the lid. He got up saying 'Excuse me' and left the room.

Deborah read the exaggerated account three times. It covered nearly a whole page. What a laugh! *Night rider case dismissed!* She must phone Olivia for a lunchtime drink. She ate her own and her father's breakfast before going out to see to the mares.

Dead Elm

'THE VOICES!' SOMETIMES HER NAME came out of the tumult. 'Jennifer!'

They turned to mumblings. Prisoners shaking iron bars.

She put her head under the pillow. She shut her eyes, yawned continuously. The yawns flashed behind her eyes like sheets.

The doctor would tell her about her dreams. The whys and wherefores.

'Obvious, my dear Jennifer.'

He glares affectionately.

His ideas come in the post. Samples: pink, blue, saffron.

'All the colours of the Australian humming-bird.'

He comes from there. Melbourne, to be precise.

'Your medical system,' he also likes to say, as if she were responsible for the failings of the National Health.

One day she said to him, 'Make me well.'

The sun shone, then, gilded the bottles on the bedside table; she marvelled at its impudence, its insistence. It was winter; she fancied summer; herself and Paul trailing their toes in the river; her legs like drums, his white and thin. He was throwing her back in the grass, putting leafy branches over her and she was looking up at him through the leaves. His head was at a rakish angle, freckled by the shadows from the willow tree above them, his face the colour and texture of seed cake.

The sun left the room which folded into its morning grey; it was winter. Yes. Then they were in the attic of the big house, sitting under the rows of summer dresses, outmoded suits, picture hats. They availed of silence. The silence spread between them like a tablecloth crisp from the laundry.

Jennifer told herself to get up; her legs, criss-crossed by heavy muscle, thundered to the floor. She sat on the bed, gazed at the wallpaper.

That had been an issue!

She had said to her mother, 'Fin-de-siècle, I think.' The shrink had said, 'Get down to it quickly. Don't think about it.' Twice he said, 'Otherwise …'

They had laughed a lot in mutual cynicism. She, cur, cur, cur; he, cho, cho, cho—until his legs got jammed under his desk.

She had succumbed and done it, or half done it. So it would always be; with little sausages of air behind the strips which were out of true.

Jennifer spent many hours with Dr Spooner; he told her his troubles.

She gazed and sank into the void in which she often spent hours at a time.

Occasionally she mumbled or called out, the words as monotonous as an accountant's who adds up his figures aloud.

Jennifer's mother, Lily, woke up in a different manner; the duvet under which she slept had fallen down and she was cold. She pulled it. She listened to the noises of Jennifer. She heard the mumblings and shiftings and longed to go back to sleep. But she had no time. She had to rise, rattle the door handle, the daily signal that was supposed to motivate her daughter into getting dressed.

'See that she's up and dressed before you go to work.'

Little laws he laid down. 'We'll fight this together,' he had said once, with an almost flirty twitch of his eyelashes.

Hearing the rattle, Jennifer reacted according to book. She

pulled on a green polo-necked sweater, her jeans, her football socks, her cowboy boots, and thundered down the passage to take up her stance in front of the gas cooker in the kitchen.

She took up her stand like an American footballer waiting for the whistle, her shoulders forward, her hands embracing her shoulders, the fingers picking at the wool of her jumper. Her body, upholstered in all its flesh, dominated the kitchen, interfered with light and space and when Lily came in and saw her daughter as usual, planted, she felt the outrage creeping on her; the domestic accoutrements appeared to bend themselves around her daughter, only the body, unmoving except for the fingers, was just then a permanent fixture.

'Take her through the door into the reception area.'

'She needs treatment.'

Jennifer laughed; her shoulders bucked. She twisted her head to follow her mother's movements, how her mother leaned round her to get the empty kettle, splashed water into it and put it on the gas, holding it down as though to encourage it to boil more quickly.

Mother and daughter stood side by side.

'I made a plan,' Jennifer said.

'Yes?'

'I'm going to see Paul and Fiona this morning.'

'Did the voices ...' Lily heard the sarcasm in her voice, tried to modify. 'Yes. On a fine morning like this. Nice. Good for you. To get out and about.'

Mother and daughter stood close then, in silence.

The gas roared.

Jennifer, removing a hand from her shoulder, ran it down her mother's dressing gown. 'It's still pretty, Mum.' The silk, rasped by her knuckles, made pools of light under the shadow of her arm.

'Her mind is perfectly lucid,' said the doctor. Who was he telling?

Dressing in her room, Lily allowed the gown to fall in a puddle at her feet. Mum? Still nice? A bare toe touched the centre of its folds; the material, slithering beneath her weight, felt like water. She set her face in softer lines; her eyes relaxed. She blew into the mirror. Her life in the looking-glass. Proof? Of what? She hurried back.

'The kettle has nearly boiled dry. Why don't you tell me to get out of the way?'

'I'm sorry, but I'm in a hurry.'

'So efficient, Mum, so severe.'

'Yes. I said I was sorry. I've three classes this morning.'

Lily lifted her arm to rest on her daughter's shoulder; she was tired. Her day of teaching ahead of her; the roomful of foggy, lugubrious teenagers instilled in her nothing less than terror every day. Jennifer's breathing dominated when Lily turned down the gas. She knew she must get away as quickly as possible before she cursed her daughter to her face.

Every morning she had to ask her had she taken her pills, while knowing how finally obnoxious the treatment was—destructive of the original persona.

There were four different kinds.

'I suppose you've taken your …'

Jennifer woke up into amusement. 'Probably.'

Lily laughed obligingly. 'That means yes?'

'What would Dr Spooner say if he heard you?'

Jennifer's lips tunnelled into her cheeks. 'Do your adolescent schoolboys stroke your legs as you chalk up theorems on the blackboard?'

'That's enough.'

Perhaps her coarseness had been exacerbated by this new Australian shrink, Lily wondered.

For her daughter's sake she had left Dublin to come and live in this unpromising English town. Partly because Jennifer's childhood friends, Fiona and Paul, twins—the two families inextricably mixed together at home—had moved here some years back. They now occupied an old house—it was a commune of sorts—which stood back from the road about a quarter of a mile the other side of town. As far as Lily knew, Jennifer had never been out to visit them. But what did Lily know? Indeed her daughter might, on some unaccounted day, have gone out there. Twice the twins had called and tried to persuade her out. But of more importance was the coinciding fact that Lily had been steered here by the reputation of the doctor in the local hospital. The chief consultant, an endocrinologist as well as a psychiatrist, who was supposed to be the best in his trade.

A nut case, in other words, who chewed continuously— his coat collar, his memo pad, his biro—with the resolution of a donkey mowing through a field of thistles.

He made magnanimous remarks about her, Lily's, patience. 'A commodity hard to come by these days.' As if it was something that went up every year with inflation.

Lily threw her egg into the sink. Perhaps there was nothing he could do. He could not, after all, shrink her daughter like a woollen vest. Nor, indeed, bring back her father.

Yes, it was Jennifer's size that mother and daughter feared equally. Neither spoke of it. With the toughening of her body fibres had seemed to come their mutual loss of ingenuity or improvisation.

Lily would look at her daughter's face which had pulped, obscuring her once neat features; the nose widened, the cheeks browned and swollen, and she found it hard not to snap at her or utter cutting words.

How petty, how awful, to judge her daughter thus.

But eventually they had learned to play. Or Jennifer had learned. Lily wasn't sure. At least the pills controlled the spiral of rage into which her daughter used to climb before she started having treatment.

Obligingly she now placed three pound notes beside Jennifer's unopened egg.

'These might come in handy,' Lily said. 'Do go ...' *Well, out...* she thought.

Jennifer heard her mother's banging of the front door, the signal for her to wait. Every morning the old woman in the house beside theirs opened her window and shook out her dishtowel. Today was like other days.

First the hands, crinkled, loaded with liver-coloured moles. Then the nose, inquisitive as a crochet-hook. Finally the grey head with the pink seam running across the scalp, the eyes transparent as petrol, searching for some new thing to see in the walls descending, ascending, or behind the net curtain opposite.

Jennifer thought her beakish look intelligent. She spoke often of luckier times, the monologue drifting across the blank space between. She was speaking now. To the air, to the shadow behind the net curtain.

The blob.

'I'm listening,' Jennifer smiled. 'Let me be your very own blob.'

Then she lost interest. While the woman still waved her dishtowel like a flag, Jennifer watched dully.

What about her, anyway? A dumb old woman who had let herself be forgotten. Like a photograph of a long-dead relation whose name was written on the back.

Time passed for mother and daughter that morning. For Jennifer it lay on her like a tent whose poles have been snatched from beneath it.

For Lily? Well, for her she had floundered emotionally amongst forty yawning teenagers rather more obviously than usual. Returning to lunch to their flat she prayed at the traffic lights.

'Dear God, let Jennifer be gone for a walk or some damn thing.'

There she was, however, in the kitchen, splayed over the table, the uneaten egg crushed symbolically beneath her weight.

Asleep, Lily hoped, as she tiptoed in. But Jennifer sat up; Lily, alarmed, said, 'Dear Jesus!'

'What did you expect? D'you know, perhaps I'm in love with Dr Spooner instead of Paul.'

'Bit of a cliché to fall for your shrink,' Lily leaned over to get some cold meat out of the fridge.

'Of course he's a lame duck, too. Do you think I have a tendency to fall for lame ducks?'

Paul? Paul and Jennifer racing like terriers up the street.

Fiona? Fiona and Jennifer giggling over their comics, sucking dirty fingers.

And now Fiona and Clive, her son, with his apricot cheeks and sewing silk hair.

Lily cut the cold meat in quarters with a steel knife. 'I wouldn't have called Paul a lame duck.'

'Most unobservant,' Jennifer said. 'Fiona rules his life. Do this, do that. Also she imagines she's my friend but she won't let me near him. And she won't let me near Clive.'

'Twins are strange creatures. Paul is rather a rare person.'

'Lily!'

'Well. Have you slept with Paul, then?'

'Not yet.' Jennifer scraped herself into a sitting position.

'Good,' Lily said. 'I mean good that you've sat up. Now I can put my plate on the table.'

'Don't be sarcastic. You know you're dying to hear the gory details.'

'I couldn't care less whether you've slept with Paul or not.'

'God, you're such a liar. Always trying to toe the doctor's line. Humour me. Anyway, for your information I've decided to take the big step today.'

'Perhaps you'd have better luck with the doctor.'

'You're in a foul mood.'

'Just tired.'

'I don't think Dr Spooner's like a shrink, really. On the other hand, do you not think his medical mind would enjoy the experiment?'

'I hadn't thought of it like that.'

'Oh yes you have. Say it. Say it.'

'Do you think Fiona minds she has no father for Clive?' Lily wanted to change the subject. 'Pass me a tomato, please.'

'Don't men like to sniff around unmarried mothers? Besides, you know damn well who Clive's father is.'

'You're gross.'

'Yes, mother.'

'For God's sake don't let's fight. Eat something.' Lily brushed the pieces of eggshell into her hand. 'And stop calling the doctor by that ridiculous name. Do you call him that to his face?'

'You are soft, Lily. Ever since Dad left me—us—you can blame him for me. Remember. Remember. He and I had something going for each other. Didn't we? We used to play games. Word games. Make up spoonerisms.'

Lily felt her pelvis contracting.

'Reading to each other. Giggling. You were jealous. Even long-suffering you were jealous.'

'This is insane.' Where were their resolutions to pamper each other?

'What did you say?'

'Oh come on Jennifer. It's crazy. You know as well as I do that your father had "left" long before he moved out.'

'Why didn't he move in with Fiona and Paul's mum?'

'Christ, don't bring that up again.'

'Ha. The dead can't answer. Their mother is dead.'

'She was my friend.' Now Lily's voice had fallen; like a fly that has buzzed too long. She would say no more. She must learn not to answer back. She left the last bit of meat on her plate.

Lily hammered her head with a hairbrush, changed her high-heeled shoes, hurled the headmaster's reports into her briefcase, wrote a cheque for the electricity and tore it loudly from the book. Clothes sprawled on chairs, table edges. The concupiscence of the looking-glass exaggerated the confusion; her face again solid as earthenware; nowhere to hide any more.

Jennifer heard her mother's banging of the hall door for the second time that day. The voices that had been quiet in the morning now began to chorus words of advice. 'The child … the child … the child …' they seemed to say. She shuddered, thinking of Fiona's advising Paul how to live his life. Against the derogation of the voices, the traffic sounds beyond the four walls were a confidence she was not invited to share; the flat was stretching itself in the empty afternoon.

Her head sagged. Her energy went from her. She yawned continuously.

Once, on her way back from the lavatory, she had strayed into her mother's room, gazed out of the window at a scene of demolition, desolation and dogs. Better view, in the long run, than what she saw across the lift-shaft division between the kitchen wall and that of their neighbour's. Out this window was industry of all kinds, people in attitudes of prosperity of mind and material. Gay dogs all. And beyond all this—the town, the hubbub—was the mighty highway, racing, unwinding like a reel of black silk ribbon.

The poll of her forehead was chilled against the window-pane. A dog pissed beyond the bulldozers, nosed paper and disappeared. A man in a tin hat turned his gammon cheeks to the winter sky.

She was walking. She was walking in her lumpy fashion with her hands still kneading the wool of her jumper. She had passed through the town and the municipal park, interrupting the thoughts of two little girls who hung to gossip on stationary swings. She was oblivious of herself in this confinement of space, yet conscious of every detail out there. She was at the end of the lane that led to Fiona's house and forced to ponder on the part of the design of the treeless avenue that had once been a matted tunnel before disease had destroyed the elms. She was a monument to the exclusion of any other. Then again she was walking, with wide steps over black puddles; the voices nudged, ran on ahead like will-o'-the-wisps: 'New endocrinologist next week ... great strides ... great strides ...'

And milk bottles were rattling; getting nearer and nearer. It was dark; mother and child and the crate of bottles were looming up on Jennifer.

'Why, Jennifer. What are you doing here? Aren't you coming up? Good to see you. Look Clive, say hullo to Jennifer. Paul's making supper. You're just in time. But wait. I have to take the bottles down to the road. The sodding milkman won't come up the avenue anymore.'

There was the rhythm of munching of an animal in the field. Jennifer was able to feel the cast of the child against her body; she was stroking his hair. It was electric, compelling.

She was disturbed by Fiona's wariness. Observing for the first time she had pierced ears. The earrings flared and went out in the dark. Clive was blundering away from her like a derailed-railway carriage. '

Yes I was coming to visit you. And Paul.'

'Go on up if you like. I won't be a minute. I'll follow.'

The sky was expanding and contracting under the full moon; the sound of milk bottles diminishing, the house hanging against the horizon.

'Yes. Into the top place where there are skylights. Why not? Oh how I need to talk. A confidante. My mother thinks only of sex. Lily's a fool. But you're not, Paul.'

'I'm busy.'

She was noticing new things about Paul, too. His face was pale, almost yellow; the curls of his reddish hair were like tricks, changing places and hiding.

'Don't sit on the table, you'll bend it.'

His chest was quite flat, like a twelve-year-old's, his shoulders like two rabbits. It was something she could sense under his anorak. But she knew, didn't she, from the old bathing trunk days, of sandcastles into which he used to wriggle his toes like sticklebacks.

And Daddy and Fiona's mummy sitting side by side in the dunes; she used to look at them; she could have killed.

Jack's Hole, the bay was called; dangerous currents.

Jennifer began to sob; her father had pulled her ear the day he left as though she were still a child.

She was up—had wandered—into Fiona's bedroom. There were two pillows on the double bed. Clive's cot was full of stuffed animals. She was waiting there…

'Never lets me near the child. Never near the child.'

There were two staircases up to the landing outside. The clever spiral one and the main; the room was directly below the attic plain. And there were many other rooms bewildered with entrances and exits.

The child was on his way up to the room. The small determined strides up the stairs. His animal leap onto the top, the uncarpeted boards echoing under his light weight. He was in the room, running into her arms, his face clear from the cold air, his hair smelling of fruit against her chin.

Clive!'

'This is the way the lady rides. Trot trot trot.'

Faster and faster she was bouncing him up and down; the wide-open window beside them was a black panel of cold air.

'This is the way the gentleman rides. Gallopy, gallopy, gallopy.'

67

'And …' She held his shoulders like an accordion in her hands swaying, swaying, swaying…

'Jennifer. It's supper. Oh. I thought Clive came up here.'
'Clive?'
Jennifer looked into the fire of Fiona's eyes; sea-green with purple dots, darker when they flashed in anger.
'Come, there's a lovely fire in the sitting room. Paul has been sawing wood all day.'
Fiona was persuading her down into the ship-shape emotions of her brother and their friends. To talk, gather round, smoke pot, by the light of the television screen, the wild fire of dead elms, sparks riding up the chimney of the baronial fireplace.

'Oh, it's an old place, all right. The whole house trembles when you walk upstairs.'
'And why do you like going there, my dear Jennifer, if you say no one wants to see you?'
'I grew up with them in Dublin.'
The doctor shaved his pencil into a fine point. 'I think perhaps you cling on to them because they are associated with a time when your father was around. People grow away from each other. Now. I'm going to ask you to join one of our therapy groups …' his words jumped around like squirrels.
'I didn't ask to come here. To this one-horse …'
'Or to be born …' Cho cho cho.
'Cur, cur, cur,' Jennifer said. 'My mother …'
'Your mother is a fine woman.'
'Paul and I did … as growing up …'
'Yes yes. But now you move on. There's more to life than climbing trees.'

'My size—'

'A malfunction of the glands which can be reversed by the latest drugs.'

His cuff caught the pencil shavings. 'When they have been fully tested … Come on the market …'

In the sitting room, a sweep of laughter. In the corridor, the noise of taps. Beyond in the kitchen, a dozen or so mouths stop chewing.

'Why Jennifer; surprise, surprise.'

Different Kinds of Love

How he loves the train; it heaves, it crashes, flying past old cow sheds, smart continuous suburbs—every line of washing a flag to the people's spiritual notion of 'same'. How he loves the feel of 'holiday'. Three days away from the dust of the office, the dull legal tomes. For twenty years now he has followed in his father's footsteps, dithered over title deeds, unravelled minor criminal offences, made wills, separated husbands and wives. His father too, still shuffling in from time to time, poking into long-forgotten cases, his poor eyes peering over the thick-lensed reading glasses as he occasionally looks askance at his middle-aged son. This son has no more made his mark than he did but he did what his father originally wanted—he followed 'one of the professions'. Only his life with Irena had mattered till she got the stroke and lost her will to speak. Irena—now lovely dumb Irena—had nothing to say to him. She sits all day by the window reading. Then when the light dies she walks to the unlit fireplace and stands there till he comes home to light the fire and cook a meal. Long ago they divided the house and father has a flat upstairs. It is a tall Wexford building, granite—the windows glint in the sun transmitted from the house across the road. Other people have moved into the suburbs but they felt no need. The old house with its troubled sounds sufficed for the three of them: memories of children's parties—brothers and sisters flying up and down the stairs—playing 'pass the parcel' and, later, 'sardines'.

It was then he had hidden first with Irena—in a dark cupboard. She had worn an organdie party frock and he had dared to touch its stiffness but not the silk of her skin. He had prayed that they would never be found—the last to be found were declared the winners. But then the magic had ended—of course—and they had looked at each other for some years — embarrassed. Suddenly at twenty-three he had met and married the daughter of Dr Moran from Arklow. A strong-willed young woman who made some changes in the house, but, no matter how she changed it, it was still the same so she ran away with a young mechanic and set up house with him in Waterford.

Irena was working then. Working in the local hospital as an administrative secretary. He had partially forgotten her— her organdie frock, her soft lips that he had never touched, her pale hands and the way in which she used move the elastic wrist-watch strap up her arm as if to show off the watch of which she was so proud. No, he had been too wrapped up in his woes even to notice her when they bumped into each other in the hotel bar. It was she who had cautiously said his name while he ordered himself a Powers Gold Label intending to retreat to the table by the fire to sit and brood.

'Martin,' she had said. 'Martin Hamilton.'

Passionately they loved after that. He would visit her in her small flat every moment they were both free. There they would count each other's bones beneath the blankets, two lost fools, as though the rest of the world had been made as silent as snow.

So for many years the fuddy-duddy dry-as-dust solicitor and the confident administrative nurse to all respects and purposes lived separate lives, he returning to sleep in his dusty house at night, she opening her curtains to let in the air that their recent laughter and love had excluded, as they excluded everything else.

Then came the stroke. He had found her one lunchtime all lop-sided on the sofa. Later in the hospital as the weeks passed she gradually regained the use of her body. She worked hard with her hands and legs, she fought like a tiger for her old strength. Soon she could walk, bend, do light tasks, but the speech was gone. He moved her into his home when she was discharged. To the world—who of course knew everything already—this was acceptable—an act of kindness, in fact, on his part. It was still Mr Martin Hamilton, Commissioner for Oaths, son of Noel Hamilton, Solr., founder of the firm, and Ms Irena Barrington, daughter of the late Ellen and Paul Barrington, Hardware Merchants, exporters and importers, 3, The Quays, Wexford, firm now long since closed.

So what was he doing now on the train? The office was undergoing a coat of paint—long overdue—and he had persuaded his seventy-eight-year-old father to take a rest, shut up shop. Hamilton and Hamilton, closed for custom for one week only.

'I am going to Dublin,' he had told Irena. She lifted her eyes from her book, a slight frown forming between her brows, but naturally she said nothing, how could she?

They were bowling into Gorey. The train bumped to a stop. No one alighted, but a few people boarded the train and it slid forward. He must have dozed because suddenly they were cruising along the Killiney cliffs, looking down onto the coastline that has so often been compared with the Bay of Naples. Certainly the purples and greys, the greens and yellows, the sweep of the hills behind, the short sea below, the white of the gulls competing with the break of the waves, for a moment brought him back through the tunnel of time when youthfulness paid its own dividend for no other reason except that of being young. He had as yet no plans except perhaps to get drunk. Very drunk for three days. A bolstered fog of drunken nothingness.

After one day he was bored, hungover. He remembered Carmel. Another distant party-girl. A large girl who had bolted through the house with his sisters and whom he had later dated occasionally for the monthly dance in the marquee at Baltimore. He had also partnered her in the mixed doubles and they had reached the semi-finals in the annual Wexford tennis-championships.

Surprised, she agrees to meet him after work. Her voice is a shock, it is quite deep with unpleasant overlaid vowel sounds. When she arrives it's another shock. He had once had a *grá* for her athletic body, her inquisitive impatient searching. But no, her expression has lost that curiosity he had found so attractive; the wide-open eyes are there all right, but now they are strained, lined by heavy make-up as though they had never seen what they should have, while yet being wary. She has fattened, her face and hands especially, and those vowel sounds he dreads.

However, he greets with a manly leap as she enters the bar, 'What'll you have?'

'I don't drink, well rarely.'

What is she thinking of him? That he is dull and balding? Or is there a flutter there too from the feathers of her youth?

'In that case, a gin and tonic and a Powers.'

'Oh no, really, just the one, then.'

Perhaps she is an alcoholic and afraid to drink, he thinks, as the barman slaps down the drinks with little courtesy.

'Here's to it,' says he, lifting his glass; they clink uncomfortably and stare.

'Well?'

'Are we not going to see *The Damned*? I told you on the phone I'm a member of the film club.'

He has long ago lost interest in 'Art' films; he does not like television even and he wonders if he can circumvent his original offer of a 'movie'.

'Are you hungry?' When she nods, he says: 'We'll have a

bite, so. There's a café up the road, I noticed. Should we risk it?'

In the café the waitress bangs about as they huddle over their chicken and chips. 'Not our night,' Martin says, looking into Carmel's mouth.

'They're very underpaid. Don't worry. I drop in here sometimes on Fridays while waiting for my train.'

'It is curious that we haven't met all these years.'

'My family moved from Wexford town long ago.'

'Ah, that explains it.'

They stretch and turn self-consciously while Carmel pours tea from the tin teapot. He squints over the menu and offers her apple-tart. Carmel pushes the last of the greasy chips to one side and asks what film he *would* like to see. He says he would prefer to go to her place for a quiet evening, 'To fill in the blanks.'

'What blanks?'

'In our acquaintan– friendship,' he mutters, 'of the past twenty years or so.'

Her face has become stiff and he feels as if a strong brush has swept his brain empty of all inventiveness.

He levels his voice: 'This place is destructive. Let's have a drink.'

'If that's what you really want I'll accompany you, but I've told you I don't drink.'

'Do you dislike me?' he asks elbowing the glass door.

'Why should I?' clearly surprised by this volte-face.

'I feel I treated you badly once.'

'You were great fun.'

What an extraordinary thing, he thinks, that he ever could have been 'fun'. He looks round at her as they walk, the curtain of disapproval is back. 'I liked you a lot,' he says, his speech beginning to limp.

The Pearse Street pub, male oriented, offers a dim lounge

as an alternative to the bar. The lounge is empty, barring one other couple and, as she sits down in the corner, Carmel looks up at him and for a moment he glimpses that long-ago curiosity which had once made his adrenalin quicken.

'Do have something,' he begs.

'No thanks, really, please. Anything. Any old thing. But not gin.'

He suddenly remembers one Seamus, grey-flannelled, debonair, with whom she knocked around while she studied typing at the tech and how he had felt contractions of jealousy each time he saw them together.

He wonders did they ever sleep together. With a pang of regret he remembers giving her an orgasm behind the tennis pavilion when the other players had all gone home.

He has ordered a double Powers and a lemonade for her and she asks him what is he thinking about.

'You.'

'In what way?'

'What happened to Seamus?'

'Oh him!' She bursts into a short loud laugh. 'I haven't thought about him for years.'

Martin suddenly thinks of Irena. How she will have no one to light the fire and that he can't sleep with her any more and how she'll only eat rubbish when he's not there to cook.

'And you,' Carmel asks, 'Are you married?'

'Me. Oh, sorry. I was just thinking of something. Betrayals actually.'

'Betrayals?'

'Never mind. Well no, I'm not married exactly. I was. But now I have a … well, never mind. Did you ever betray anyone irrevocably?'

'I've lied to my parents.'

Martin shouts at the barman, 'Another large Powers.'

'Why don't you say "please"?'

'Because I'm unreasonable.'

'You're mad!'

'An odd word.'

'I don't understand you.'

'Sorry to sound abrasive but can I fuck you tonight?'

'No need to shout at me or the barman. He's not responsible for your greed.'

'That's another funny word.' And you haven't answered my question.

'The answer is no. At least not tonight.'

Martin feels a spiral of anger reaching for his throat.

'There won't be another night. I'm going home tomorrow.'

'That proves it.'

His anger subsides at once. Poor naive forty-three-year-old Carmel, knowing nothing of the weary world.

'You're right,' he says, 'I'm both greedy and somewhat mad. I imagined we could pick up the threads right away. Of cornflowers and tennis courts, twisted ankles and … and … well you occupied a small sunny corner in my dismal post-college years.'

But she is overcome, jumps up knocking over the remnants of his drink, her coat, handbag, gloves, gathered to her like an old woman fleeing from a mobster. The door swings in the night air. As he mops the table, her passage is lost amongst the city-sounds as are the saffron summers of his past.

Little worms of light come through the curtains as he hurries along the street to his house. In the sitting room Irena stands at the mantelpiece. There is a smell of stale urine and a dark spread in the carpet at her feet.

'Irena,' he gathers her up. Her mind is withdrawn and still as he races upstairs. In the bathroom he undresses her quickly.

She makes no move either to prevent or help, just sits limp on the edge of the bath while the water widens in the tub. As he places her in the bath he noses her stale hair and realises with a terrible agony that he hasn't seen her naked for years. 'Irena,' he mutters, over and again as he soaps between the folds of her body, her pubis like a dark plant, a darkening between her thighs, her ankles somewhat swollen from the long hours of standing.

Sometimes she looks with despair at her wasted body which should be rounded and hopeful, and when she is lifted and dried he bundles her into her bedroom while he demonically changes sheets and makes the bed.

At last they are together, his cold thighs warming against hers. He lies on one elbow, stroking her cheek, her shoulder. He tells of his betrayal and his failure to seduce. He laughs with rueful anguish at his recent bullishness.

'Can you imagine,' he says, 'she called me both greedy and mad. But I am not mad, Irena, I am not mad.'

Out-patients

'THIS WAY. PLEASE. NO. NOT YOU, DEAR.' The orderly beckoned to Nina. 'You,' she said. Her voice dropped, not sure whether Nina was next in the queue. Nina held the left elbow in her right fist taking care not to jolt it.

'Have you given your name, dear?'

'No. Not yet.'

'Oh,' the orderly said. 'Then you'd better sit down again.'

Nina sat down on the wooden seat. She could see the nuns bustling around beyond the glass partition; they moved separately from each other, some with papers in their hands, all their faces polished. Behind the partition there was no sound; mute sisters of charity.

Hack away the sleeve as the arm swells! But they're in a hurry and won't notice.

Jesus! The bastard's broken it this time! What can she tell them, these remote women? That she is a lousy wife and gets beaten up every so often?

So she can't admit it? Must she lie, make up a new story each time, each one more improbable than the last, in order to maintain the core of the myth that marriage works? So that, as society believes, the woman is, finally, to blame?

Is that it?

Nina was cold, undernourished, too lightly clad; she was trying not to shiver or laugh or annoy the woman beside her.

78

She looked occasionally into the area beyond the glass partition and wondered would the nuns suddenly gather their papers into their arms and stride towards them—the sick, the destitute.

But she did laugh and the woman, or rather girl, beside her crouched low and shook her head; the pale hair rose and fell like cotton on her cheeks.

'They take their time,' she said.

Nina read: NO LOITERING. Like the NO SMOKING notice it had been, always would be, ignored. They hung around and smoked, their hands curled round the cigarettes, wisps of smoke trailing through the fingers. When the nuns came they would stamp the cigarettes and put the stubs in their pockets.

She knew it was lucky it was her left arm that he had hit for half an hour. Or it had seemed like that. It had been dole day and he had been drinking all afternoon; he was in that sodden destructive mood that came on him every Tuesday, and when he saw Frank who had just called in he began.

He'd simply said, 'Go!' and Frank had gone and Brendan had picked up the axe handle. Useless her trying to escape, shielding her face with her forearm which took the punishment. She'd run round the room, ducked under the table, shouting, Stop, please stop!

But it *was* lucky it was her left arm. She thought and thought about the sewing she needed to do; the middle child, poor kid, no button on his coat and off to school in rubber boots.

How did other mothers keep their children neat, spotless? Why couldn't she? That time Frank came and sat beside them on the canal bank she'd been ashamed of their pale grubby faces, the middle one, again holding his coat shut with one hand and fishing for minnows with the other. But a short moment of happiness had come on her when he had put his notebooks on the grass and touched her shoulder.

'You don't say very much,' he had said. 'But you make me feel intelligent.'

'What a strange thing to say,' had she said? Or perhaps, 'But you are, aren't you?' At any rate they had looked into the canal which was clear and still as a photograph till he'd let go her shoulder to stir the water with a stick and splinter their reflections, and she thought he must have been embarrassed when he touched her but the touch of his hand on her arm had changed the day, the whole week, even.

The nun had come and was leading the girl beside her down the corridor. It would be her turn soon and she must have her story ready. Last month it had been a rigmarole about slipping in the wet yard and …

She looked up at the nun who had returned.

'Name?'

A biro was poised over the writing pad.

'Nina Sheridan.'

The few details checked, the nun looked at her arm. A precise glance, 'How did you get this?'

And now the story must run its course. Nina remembered some half-prepared sentences: 'I was diving off a jetty at Seapoint and my arm hit off a rock.'

'Have you children?'

'Four.'

'And where were your children when you were diving into the sea?'

'Playing in the sand.'

'Alone?'

'Yes. They were quite safe. You see …'

Nina stood now before the nun; anger had begun to run down her chest. 'Yes,' she shouted.

'Sit down,' the nun said.

It was all wasted, the anger, the accelerated heartbeat; the nun had walked away and Nina had to sit again, alone this time except for a copy of *The Word* which lay, half open, on the seat beside her.

She would check her fury by reading *The Word*, a magazine that told you facts about people worse off than yourself, as opposed to women's magazines which left your mind open to fantasy. She slid her hand over the cover, uneasy, for as yet she was not prepared to admit to the lack of fight that had reduced her own life in essence to the status of some of the women from whom circumstances had removed the last grain of hope. But she was saved from opening it by the return of the nun. She bore upon her with that assertiveness that seemed even worse then than the anger that had now quite left her, or worse, even, than the continuous throbbing of her arm.

'First visit?'

'I was here three months ago with a broken nose.'

The nun looked away.

'I'm accident prone.' Now she could begin to laugh, to ignore.

'I forgot to ask your address.' Nina's arm was picked up and dropped like a stone being quickly replaced on a nest of slugs. The shock of pain lodged under her armpit. Tears burnt.

'I'll have to find your file.'

Nina worried about the babies; would Brendan mind them or would he just go out and leave them alone?

'Get up, get up for God's sake, you've broken my arm!' Had she said that with authority? Or, 'I have to go to the hospital. Mind the children!' Please? Hardly!

There were others lined up now, not least an oldish man with all the emblems of the wino—mac stained from nights on the streets, a man who could never be astonished again, an old rag of a bandage on his hand—here for a dressing, a bit of warmth, a secure telling off.

Nina was invaded by coldness. She wished she could afford paper nappies. For how could she wring out pissy blankets with one broken arm?'

'You may follow me.' The nun came and went and Nina

followed as she strode ahead as though in grand opera. In a small room two patients were already seated. Their expressions laid back, they held charts in their hands. One woman had a plastercast down her leg, which left her five toes bared, inquisitive, impervious to the cold. She wondered how long a fracture would take to heal in her own case? A month? Six weeks? The comedy might continue indefinitely, for how could she take in typing now? Yes, until the fracture knitted they would have to beg Brendan for some of his dole, or steal—and not for the first time. She laughed, addressing the woman with the broken leg.

'Have you been here long?'

'I don't know what they're at.'

'Are you an In-patient?'

The woman got painfully up, she had been called to the next stage, the pre-X-ray room, to queue again, presumably. The orderly in charge of her turned to Nina.

'You for X-ray?'

'I think so.'

'Have you got your card?'

'No.'

He herded out the woman on crutches. Through the other door, the first nun entered.

'Where's your chart?'

'I haven't got one.'

The nun clicked her heels like a soldier on parade.

'They keep doing that.'

Nina sat on with the second woman who had obscured herself behind a sheet of patience and the nun disappeared once more.

She would give up smoking, save up, buy shoes—those nice Clark's sandals—for the middle child. And walk out to meet Frank on the canal bank, lie in the sun, stir the water, talk of Brendan's cruelty; she became lost in the fraud of fantasy.

'Here's a card!'

The Word tucked under her bad arm, Nina took the card.

'I can't find your chart.'

They couldn't take the card away now, she thought. She spoke to the other woman.

'At least I have an identification. Perhaps things will speed up.'

'I doubt it,' the woman spoke undramatically. 'They can change their minds if they like.'

'But they have to X-ray me now.'

'Don't be too sure about that.'

Two nuns entered at last to bring them to the final room.

There the row of patients were mostly in regulation dressing gowns. Their faces were sliced from their bodies by a sly ray of sunshine. Relentless sunshine, showing up the illnesses on each face, making everyone look worse, even, than they were. She counted them—twelve. The radiographer must have gone for her break.

Would Brendan feed the baby, she wondered, looking the length of a TWA poster; the girl, chocolate-faced, sipped a blue drink under the shade of a striped umbrella; she was being watched by a young man, his chunky face animated by lust, his skin a lighter shade than the girl's—the colour of cardboard.

But now they were moving; the queue was diminishing; the radiographer must be back from the coffee break. Had she eaten ginger biscuits?

The patients straightened their features each time a nun passed, but Nina, not knowing why, could not do so; her lies, her self-protection, created an area of secrecy beyond which others could not travel. This she created in herself, aware of its lack of value, good sense.

She thought only of the button missing from the child's coat, even forgetting Frank or her husband, Brendan, the man with whom she sometimes felt she had traded her sanity.

The card fell out of her hand, lay at her feet; a discarded

bingo card—squares and numbers—Nina Sheridan, upside down and married. Respectable ...

'Mrs Sheridan!' How had the room emptied so suddenly? The few magazines sliding from the bench; the woman at her typewriter relaxing; a little coffee spilled on the saucer of an empty cup.

'You may go in now.'

She bent for the card to tuck into *The Word*. Careful again not to jolt her arm, aware of the lifting throb as she walked to the door of the X-ray room.

'Did he clout you?'

'Not once, but many times.'

No trace of disapproval on the radiographer's face. As she bent, the clean overall swung open over the fresh cotton of her dress. 'Men are beasts!' She smiled, played with her machines. 'I'll try not to hurt you. You've had a long wait.'

Now Nina could state: 'Everyone's in the same boat.'

'There's no same boat about it. It's the old formula. Take away people's self-reliance. Tell them nothing. Then we give them the soft sell. Twenty, thirty times a day.'

She brushed Nina's fingers. 'Try to straighten them.'

A half-moon with the hand was crushed back with the effort.

'Sorry.'

'Don't apologise. Just lie there with your arm on the paper. I won't hurt you,' she said again.

The shutters of the machine swished.

'That's great. Fine.'

So she had shut her eyes, she knew, because the face above her swung like a coin in the distance, too far away to touch, for she would have drawn her fingers like a pencil over the contours of the mouth had she been able to reach.

'Perhaps I slept.'

The radiographer held out a larger than foolscap envelope.

'Where do I go now?'

'Home.'

'The fracture?'

'Don't worry.'

'But the X-rays? May I not see … I mean …'

'I think you are the last this morning. Take your time.'

The radiographer was holding the door open, watching the tread of the patient's feet into the empty shoes; *The Word* was on the floor again, cover page folded back. A Somali infant stood naked, navel protruding like a rotten grape.

'I dropped my magazine. Or rather it's not mine. It's a good magazine, isn't it?'

Love is so fleeting, Nina thought. So inadequate.

The Hairdresser

LONG AGO THEY HAD PAINTED THE HOUSES. Pale pastel shades—mauves, pinks, greys. The estate had expanded up Trevor's Hill, across the old sheep-field, curling back down like an anvil until it seemed that the mountain had grown a second crust. Attempts to divert the streams had failed and water ran freely into the residents' gardens and rotted the foundations of the houses.

Paint cracked, window frames warped; there seemed no wisdom in the continuous building of new dwellings, but, after the last of the city clearances, the Local Authority brought out their trucks, their cranes, their earth-movers and parked them in the road that ran directly through the estate till it could run no more and ended, T-shaped, beneath the higher slopes.

Electric wires, even pylons blew down in the storms and were seldom repaired so the estate lay mostly in darkness during the winter. There were strange happenings behind those closed doors at night. Many of the middle-aged women, whose husbands had taken off or been gaoled during the nineties, took in men—those who roamed the country homeless—with whom they shared their bed and welfare payments. Their sons, who were also mostly incarcerated in some institution or other, and many of their daughters, too, left them free and lonely. Occasionally a daughter would return with a new brood. This accounted for second-generation children. Those men came and went; domestic unease, lack of money, young children crowding and squabbling, frequently drove them out after a few months.

The women did their best and it was not unusual to see a middle-aged woman perched on her roof, trying to pin over bits of plastic or rope up a piece of guttering.

Like many another family, Mona and her mother inhabited one of the highest buildings, therefore victim of the worst winter weather, and they spent many hours plastering, drying, mending window frames and replacing slates. But apart from this they were not run-of-the-mill, because the daughter was one of the few people—if not the only one—who attended secondary school. A rather plain girl with dry, ribbed hair and a boxy figure, she was something of a scholar. Her mother was a gaunt angular woman with fierce energy. Unlike the other women she attracted a certain type of man, more chaotic, more unprincipled than the average, who would enjoy her passionate responses but who wearied quickly and took his revenge with calculated cruelty.

To Mona, her mother gave the recurring excuse that 'they were safer with a man about'. Mere excuse, of course, because the marauding gangs 'cased' every house and in theirs there was little or nothing to steal. The video was the usual target and they had long ago sold theirs, sold almost everything, in fact. The house was bare of furniture except for the minimum requirements. In the kitchen, which was also the sitting room, there was a table, covered in a thin plastic cloth, a few upright chairs, and in the bedrooms there were mattresses on which lay bundles of matted blankets. Only Mona's room was spotless. Her fastidious nature forbore squalor of any kind, and to this room, as soon as she had cooked the dinner, she would retire, her lesson books spread before her, a stub of a candle lighting the immediate circle on the floor, and with her stiff hair tied behind her neck she would concentrate on her studies to the exclusion of all else.

For some weeks now a new man had established himself in their household. Although he combined all the complexities and evil ways of his forerunners, he was as yet an unknown quantity to Mona. Her mother, forever alert, listened to his speeches—for he made speeches all day long—claiming an intellectual monopoly on all subjects under the sun. This irked Mona who had a fine mathematical brain and knew that he was often wrong in his summing up of various points of social or political argument. However, for the sake of her mother she held her peace.

Today she had decided to scrub the lino. As she scrubbed and picked between the cracks she was conscious of his saturnine gaze following her around in between bouts of exclamations at the latest atrocities committed by the latest governments, snippets of which he read from the newspaper.

Mona scrubbed. The man stared, rustled his paper, sniffed back a lozenge of water from the end of his nose. His eyes, still as glass, were his most unsettling feature. She rose in confusion eventually; there were rings of mud on the knees of her stockings.

'Why don't you kneel on a bit of newspaper?' he asked, looking down at her legs as if she were a yearling in the ring.

'Ah, shut up,' Mona for once lost her temper. 'If you'd shift your arse I'd get on more quickly.'

All this time her mother was sitting on the edge of her chair, watching him with the air of one who waits for a child to take its first few steps.

'Don't be rude,' she said, her voice rusty from smoking.

Mona went to the sink to wring out her cloth; she looked round at him, sizing him up once again. There was madness there, she felt, in his posture, his teeth grinding, the occasional bouts of pacing; he was leaning over now, elbows on knees, his stained overcoat folded back like the open page of an almanac; his hands were gyrating as though he were shuffling a pack of cards. He had strangely delicate hands: his fingers tapered into neat girlish nails; yet he had huge tense shoulders. His face was stippled and pocked from long hours spent in the open. Looking at him now left her cold and sick. Yes, this man was not simply like the others—ruthless, fighting for survival; there were qualities within him, seams of impatience and rage that were beyond his control. Her outburst had annoyed him and she wished she had controlled her temper; she had witnessed his anger once already and it had seemed to lift out of him with inhuman urgency. Yet, far from antagonising her mother, his rages seemed to make her more submissive, more caressing, more loving than ever. Or perhaps she sensed the danger; Mona wasn't sure.

When they were alone she tried to warn her mother, but the latter, touching her own brow with the hand of lover and with her other hand taking Mona's, said, 'Don't worry, darling. It will all be over one day.'

Winter crawled; snow came and went. It was no longer possible to patch the roof, so they caught the water in buckets placed under the worst of the leaks. On a sleety February afternoon, Mona, returning wearily from her long journey back from school—it was dole day and they had bought cider—found them both slightly drunk, sitting by the fire—one more kitchen chair had been burnt—and there was a glow of frivolity between them. But on her entry he addressed her rudely, finishing up by shaking his fists and saying 'You're a nasty piece of work,' Mona snapped back, 'You're a fucking creep, yourself.'

He laughed and held out his glass for more cider.

Her mother rose, picked up the flagon, and poured the cider straight into his eyes.

The kitchen exploded. He jumped to his feet and went at her, got her on the ground, his fists round her neck, tables and chairs went flying. His delicate fingers—those lovely fingers—closing, closing on her mother's throat. With all her strength Mona kicked him from behind and he let go, roaring obscenities and trying to wipe his eyes with his sleeve. Her mother pulled herself up, screaming, apologising, begging for 'another chance'. But he was up and heading for the door, his large frame bent like a sickle, his arms stiffly held from his body. He banged out of the house. The stricken women stood face to face as though hoping for a message that would never come.

Then her mother strained after him.

Mona grasped her mother's jumper. 'No, no, Mammy, let him, let him go.'

'But I must,' her mother said, 'save him from the police.' She slipped out of her jumper like a snake shedding its skin and she too had run into the night.

The cold mountain air crept into the hall; gusts ran under the mat, up her legs, as Mona shouldered the door shut. She stood for a while, knowing now that her life was beyond the ken of the two people out there. Who was she now? Mona the lucky one, she used to call herself, the only member of the family to forestall the fate that had swallowed up the rest of them—one brother killed in a hit-and-run, another in and out of Mountjoy, a sister killed by an abortion in England, another sister who had quite disappeared. But long ago she had made a pact with herself: to work and work, to use her ability to study, to use her interests that lay beyond the hinterland of misery into which she had been born so that one day, one far-off day, she would take her mother and herself away from this no-man's territory where rats and dogs got a better living than they did. Another thing she'd promised herself was that she would never have anything to do with men, she would never allow her neat parts to be touched by the opposite sex, she would never succumb to the martyrdom of sexual love. In the estate, children gave birth to children, women were already grandmothers in their thirties. But she, Mona, trod a different path. Or did she? Should she now just pack her bags, go, too, into the recondite night, join the packs of girls and boys, small criminals, who got by 'doing cheques' or robbing the rich suburbs on the other side of the city?

But no. She must give it one more try.

She climbed the stairs, the re-lit candle dripping hot wax over her hand. In her room her books, her friends, all stacked neatly, were suddenly strangers, strangers like the two people who had recently fled into the unyielding night. She went on her knees, taking each book and fondling it. The ones she cared for most, those on quantitive and applied mathematics, she held longingly, opening them, smoothing the pages. But it was no use; they denied the half of her that was her pride. She threw them from her, went to the window, hoping she'd see her mother returning alone. But the street was dark, the houses down the hill derelict as an unused railway station. She left the window open and sank down on the bed.

A little while later she heard them; they came into the hall. They were speaking in low tones; the fight had been patched up and Mona knew that once again she'd act as though nothing had happened. Get wearily up, shop, make the dinner, return to her room and make some sort of a fist of studying.

She went downstairs; a rat or a mouse scuttled at her feet; she was used to the rodents so she kicked out at it and threw on her coat.

In the shop she would spend the few shillings that she had—money she had earned from her better-off student friends, the ones she helped with their homework. Most of her mother's dole went on cigarettes and drink and lasted for about a day. So it was up to her to keep them for the rest of the week, eking out her money on bits of food that kept them barely alive.

There was so little spending in the neighbourhood that frequently the thin girl at the cash desk wasn't at her post and Mona often edged out without paying. She prayed that it would be so, now, as she slipped into the darkness.

She skirted the heaps of rubble, piles of sand that had been there for years. There was no street lighting so she had to use her memory in order to avoid the worst puddles, and even so her shoes filled up with icy water. The journey to the shop usually took about twenty minutes—it was over a mile away—and, as it was nearly six, Mona began to run.

The fierce cold of that day was the one thing that stuck in Mona's memory above all else. How dirty papers had flared up in front of her feet as she'd run the last few paces home; how the unending gale had pierced her chest and how she had clasped her inadequate coat collar round her chin. It had always been difficult to get the key to work properly—it had been badly cut and one had to twist it this way and that in order to slot it in, and it had seemed to take longer than usual, as her white fingers grappled with the Yale, and finally with the help of the wind the door blew in and a glass fell at the end of the passage—a glass of dead flowers—and water dripped quickly onto the floor. At first she had not seen her mother; the man had gone from the kitchen and Mona assumed they had gone upstairs to continue their moments of reparation.

So Mona had begun to unwrap the meat before she saw the blood; in fact it was when she was about to throw the plastic wrapping into the rubbish bin that her eyes lit on the dark expanding pool. And before the horror had fully struck her, her first thought had been that the body contains eight pints of blood—a gallon—and that this is what will now run over the floor, sink into the cracks of the lino, make everything red and slimy. Yes, he had slit her throat with the kitchen knife and left the body curled up in a heap, half-hidden by the piece of oil cloth that dripped down over the back of the table.

But the years had now passed. That murder had just become another legend in the estate, one of the many legends of killings and rapings. The football pitch, which had once been a place of recreation, had now become a graveyard for the people who died daily of diseases brought on by malnutrition and were bundled into the ground. There were thousands of dogs who crowded the 'funerals' and who, when night came, dug up the corpses and ate them. Soon the people had ceased to care and left the bodies unburied for the scavengers. Everyone pretended they had not eaten human flesh.

And what of Mona?

After her mother's murder the madman had disappeared and was never found—no doubt he had holed up with some other lonely woman. Mona had left school and gone to work in a better-off estate ten miles nearer the city, as a hairdresser's assistant. She had continued to live in the same house, which was now neat and tidy, the roof well-patched and the gutters straightened. She had no friends and seldom went out after dark. But as the years passed and the country fell more and more deeply into the well of poverty, her job folded and for want of something to do she took over the old hardware shop and turned it into an establishment of her own. Nobody could pay, so Mona accepted anything they could offer, from watercress—which still proliferated in the hills—to bits of food stolen from the inner suburbs or raided from the shops that had managed to survive the 'starving eighties'.

People would do anything to get their hair fixed by Mona; it was the only entertainment left to them; women, men and children flocked in, happy to queue for hours, their absent expressions momentarily lit by narcissistic anticipation. Yes, there was nothing for them to do; the revolution that everyone had hoped for had never evolved. The only way in which they might have expressed themselves would have been to fight the gangs of vigilantes who held the city in a grip of violence. But that would have meant a long trek into town and people were too underfed to face it. So Mona cut and dyed and permed from nine to six; the mathematician in her enjoyed the definition of a pleasant hair-do. She had grown gaunt, like her mother, and she was a strange sight behind her broken windows as she measured and sized up individual hairs. She would assess the sweep of a customer's locks with the same fixed expression in her eyes as that which her mother had used to pin down her menfriends.

The smell from the football pitch would waft in from outside while people admired their reflections in the mirror; at times the purple fissures and cracks enhanced or disguised their gaunt features, their hollow eye-sockets or their sagging skin.

Mona didn't care about all this but she cared, oh so deeply, about her own expertise; if a person moved his head suddenly she'd get into a stifling rage. One day, she knew, she would kill one of her customers with the scissors, she would murder them as cold-bloodedly and as bloodily as her mother had been murdered; she'd clip them up inch by inch, first the ears, then she'd shove the scissors up their nostrils and so on and so forth.

Cedric Dear

I AM TRYING NOT TO LOOK AT MY FATHER; he has changed so much since I saw him six years ago. The old memory is gone; he didn't know me when I arrived. Mother's the same, of course. More tyrannical, if anything. She's usurped his place at the head of the table and is doling out the food as if she was about to poison us both. Well, she was always in the ascendancy and possibly he just woke up one morning and decided, That's enough.

I wonder.

He looks bad.

Never a big man, he's shrunk into a little gnome; his face is coarse like lichen. And his voice. His voice used to be a thin aristocratic whine, but now it's just a whimper.

He looks hungry, too; she's probably trying to starve him as well.

'More cauliflower, father?'

'No thanks,' mother breaks in. But he's holding out his hands pitifully.

And he shifts about all the time; twirling in his chair as if hunted by evil; what weariness of the spirit has reduced him to this absent state?

And Theresa? Theresa whom I always loved beyond measure? She's failed too. A loving humorous person. But she has grown stiff and white; tiny as well.

Theresa! I cry out to her silently. You saved me so many times when I was young. But perhaps I don't appeal to her now. Now that I've grown fat and successful. Yes, when year after year I'd return from my travels, heartsore from my interminable love affairs, she'd say: 'Come on, Cedric, forget your masculine pride. Things will work out in the end.' We used to walk in the last light of day, looking down over Bray Head, watching the cotton-white houses turn to umber and then light up like fireflies all over the hill.

I used to come home every summer; perhaps she is hurt that I stayed away so long.

She and my father are dying. Inch by inch they fade before me.

'A nice wine, mother!' I hold my glass against the candlelight; it swims rose-red.

'When I heard you were coming ...' Her strident tones make the candle flames bend over...

'Yes, mother,' I interrupt. 'I have been very remiss ... But you must understand that my most recent researches have kept me scurrying round the four corners of the earth. I have come up with some interesting...'

'Have you, Cedric dear?'

'Yes, mother. My latest work has been highly praised by the connois—'

'I'm so glad for you, Cedric dear.'

'More roast beef, Mrs Stewart?' Theresa holds the dish of meat while mother rakes abundance onto her plate, stabbing her mouth with the table napkin.

'What about father?' I say stupidly.

He gives a little cry; a rat scenting danger.

'Don't encourage him, for heaven's sake.'

While she talks she is piling morsels of gristle and fat on the edge of her plate. My appetite recedes as I watch her wolfing down her food.

Theresa picks up the decanter and pours a little more wine into my glass.

'You are not eating much,' she says.

Do I scent mischief? 'What about you? Have you eaten?'

She nods.

There was a time when we had about four maids. I used to stir up minor revolutions below stairs every time I came home. They expected me to describe my travels as if I were recounting the tales of the Arabian Nights, with all the sexual details embroidered with scarlets and mauves. So I made it all up. Only Theresa knew of the Mrs Perys and the Mrs Whitworths and the stolen love-making in sordid hotel bedrooms, the passages smelling of urine and houseboys giggling outside.

No wonder my wife left me.

No wonder Theresa doesn't love me any more.

'Would you like a little cheese, Cedric dear?'

Without waiting for my answer, mother sweeps her arm across the table and grabs father's sleeve. He has just reached for his glass.

'I think we'd better clear, Theresa.' And then she shouts as if he weren't in the room. 'Wine doesn't agree with him any more; very little goes a long way with old people.' Her glass has been refilled several times during this embarrassing meal.

I cannot defend him because I cannot defend myself; I can only adopt an attitude of reserved politeness towards her. I wish that Richard, my younger brother, were here to take the onus of pretence off my shoulders.

The meal is finished. Theresa slowly stacks the plates on the sideboard, and father, trying to rise, has knocked his hand against his glass which sways dangerously.

'You see, dear?' Mother expands villainously as she watches the old man grapple with the effort of walking. He puts his clenched fist on the folding leaf of the table before making a dive for the door.

'He can manage perfectly when he wants,' she says to my anxious hovering by his side.

'Can you manage, mother?'

She, now, is having difficulty in getting up, but finally erect she stalks after father, clip clip with her cane on the carpet. Monstrous, indefatigable woman!

'The whole world is coming to a standstill, Theresa.'

'Your father has failed very much, only these last few months.'

'He is very old, of course, but I never expected the Protestant will to give in so easily. Punctuality, grim duty alone, you'd think, would have preserved his senses to the end.'

'She has him beaten, I'm afraid.'

'Of course I suppose I knew she would. And she has Richard. He never cared much for Richard.'

'You left us alone a long time, Cedric,' she says, having removed all the squalor of the meal, as she bends over to wipe the table.

'If it were only you here, I'd come home every six months.'

'No, you wouldn't.'

'My wife left me, did mother tell you? Yes. Shortly after my last visit home.'

'I don't blame her.'

'You are hard!'

'You knew it would go like that. And your young men?'

'They are both in the States with her.'

'I suppose they correspond?' she asks, sly.

'No, of course they don't. Well, once in a blue moon. They are Americans and as such they have escaped back into their cocoon.'

'It is in the nature of things.'

'You are so loyal, Theresa, to have stayed with the old people all these years.'

'I'm old.'

'So am I.'

'You're fifty-four.'

'I wouldn't like to have you about when I'm trying to impress some lady.'

'Are you still at that?'

'Oh, Theresa, my love.'

'Come,' she says and leads me to the window.

She pulls back the dark velour curtains and opens the casement wide. 'See!'

The wind has increased; it embraces us as we stand looking over the bay. The two palms wave their semaphore leaves. But the wild night is warm, comforting, with the strong smell of eucalyptus.

She closes the window abruptly.

'Now, go and talk to them. We'll have time for a walk, tomorrow.'

'Are you able for the hill?'

She doesn't answer and, as I cross the room, the glass rattles in the window-panes and I know that the frayed edges of the jig-saw will soon have fallen into place.

Father stands by the standard lamp, the only illumination in the drawing room. There are no smiles for me in the shadows of this room. This is the room where my worst moments were spent, where we were brought in one by one to kiss our parents good night, when visitors would view us like zoo animals.

'There you are, dear. Where would you like to sit?'

The fire is like a furnace and mother's brick-red face reflects the flame. 'Mother, where does father usually sit, now? Does he still sit at the window every night? Father! Will I take you over to the window?'

'Wha'?' The unfinished monosyllable tortures me. When

I lift his arm it weighs on my spirit. It is so light; it's as if there is no flesh in the sleeve. His old raglan coat still hangs in the hall. Does he ever put it on now, I wonder.

Always he would take a walk after supper, and shovelling himself into his coat would call in his glorious whine: 'Come along, Towser, come along, little fellow.' The dog, of course, is dead and hasn't been replaced.

I negotiate the dangerous undulations on the carpet. The lamp flex trails across the floor. 'Careful, now … There …'

He won't sit down. He stares vacantly through me.

'I went to Dubrovnik, last year, Father.' I try to jog his memory. Once he went there long ago and returned exuberant with the knowledge that the comparison between Killiney Bay and the Dalmatian coast was accurate; Bernard Shaw's famous dictum. He used to say constantly, 'I know because I saw for myself.' But no, it's useless. His mind is extinguished like a dead coal; no spark to ignite any more.

The chintz cushions puff under mother's weight as she leans back in the sofa. If I could turn the photograph of myself back to front I could march out of their lives forever. But there I am, five years old, a small unbeautiful face, large hostile eyes. I'm dressed in a miniature Norfolk jacket and knickerbockers for the occasion; a red setter gazes into my face. I remember the dog, a photographer's prop; and the photographer, for that matter, his obsequious manner. The photographs of Richard are more rewarding. Richard with bat and ball squint-eyed in the sun. Richard in profile on a tall horse with a docked tail. Richard on the tennis court taking a swipe at a ball. A bit blurred, this one. I probably took it myself with my box Brownie. I certainly took this one: my two dead sisters. Mary on the swing with Joyce on her knee. Poor flat-breasted Mary. She already has that look of grim resignation on her features that was so pronounced when she grew up.

Only happy on a horse. One cold December morning she

went, with father, to a meet at Calary. The story goes that as she was mounting her mare a hound loosed itself from the pack and darted across the bog road in front of it. The mare reared in fright and she was thrown backwards onto a stone. Apparently she lay there for quite a while in the confusion of horses' hooves and baying dogs until someone realised what had happened.

I was away at the time. I remember I was in Djakarta. I was standing under the pink and lavender terraces beneath the countless seated buddhas, the eternal heat hammering down, when a small boy arrived panting up the steps with a telegram in his hands …

But of Richard's twin, James, there is no photograph. James went off to the island of Mauritius, settled down with a dark lady and ceased to write home. So they took away his photograph. James, without record, is wiped off the slate.

'You must be so sad about your boys.'

'They are men, now, mother.'

My half-American sons loafing about, leaving ash all over my notes.

'Richard is sending his son, Patrick, to Trinity this term…'

A small, pointed tooth cushions down her lower lip. 'Such a pity.'

'What is?' I say after a vacant moment.

'That he didn't get into Cambridge.'

'Yes, I suppose it is. But he'll be company for you. Richard himself, you told me in your last letter, has applied for a consultancy in Dublin.'

I am really thankful that Richard can give her what I am incapable of. I wonder if she can find any more threads to sew into her lack of maternal feeling for me. My divorce was a tremendous pleasure for her, of course; but that's a while ago. The actuality of my being remains a mystery to me. Is it possible I once lay naked in her womb? Embarrassing.

Knotted into silence, my father still stands by the window. One demented fist has grasped the faded chintz of the curtains; he is holding it tightly like a baby holding a comforter. His head wags back and forth. Suddenly, with a convulsive movement his body swivels towards me. Without realising it I have picked up the photograph of Mary and Joyce and he has seen it. Somehow this action of mine has pierced the apathy. I am holding Mary's photograph in my hand. I hold it out to him.

'I took this, do you remember, father?'

I catch him as he darts across the room and, as I tumble him backwards into a chair, he whimpers, 'Little thing … little thing …' clawing at my face with his nails.

'No, father, no. Please don't do that.'

'Give it, give it…'

I can barely hear his whine. 'Here, father. Take it. You hold it.'

I have to tear his hands from my face as I hand him the photograph, but his anguish, his anger, are spent. The photograph slides between us onto the floor and it lies there as I slowly straighten up.

I feel quite weak; my legs have gone cold and moist. Without picking it up or glancing at my mother I find myself flying up the stairs, and it's not till I reach the top landing that I stop to wonder what I'm at. I'm reduced to nervous hysteria by a single word from my senile father. A highly successful art-dealer, with numerous friends, three erudite volumes on the history of Far Eastern art to my credit, fifty-four years old with a heavy paunch and a heavy wallet, yet I'm as naked as a fish in a river between two high banks when I return to this house.

I'm in such a state, I can't stop trembling and I'm obliged to sit down on the top stair to calm my thoughts. If I go over my day perhaps some order can be created out of this chaos.

After I met Ian Niesdan and ironed out our difficulties over the carriage of the canvasses, I had lunch. In the Shelbourne. I then took the train to Killiney—at least after I had spent an hour or two in the National Gallery—and it was dusk when I stepped off the train and a high wind was banging against the flimsy stays of the metal bridge and making them rattle. I could hear the signals rattling too and the singing of the telephone wires, the hum of the sleepers. Along the sea road I enjoyed the buffeting of the wind and the noise of the sea crashing on the pebbled beach. At the foot of Kilmore Hill I crossed the road to take another look at the sea. I was struck by how old and winterish it looked this autumn night. There was a solitary rowing boat moored near the white rock, desperate to be gone. I watched the wild streaks of red and black in the sky fade into grey wads of cumuli, the soft west wind tearing them apart and reshuffling them till the horizon of sea and sky were one. Slowly and pleasurably I climbed the hill; I ran my hand along the laurel hedge caressing the fuchsia bushes, imagining the individual black and purple flowers dancing like ballerinas. Somehow or other I expected the dog to welcome me, but, of course, as I've said, he was put down a year or so ago.

Mother opened the door and the wind raced in like a herd of cattle.

'There you are, Cedric dear.'

I didn't see father at first when I entered the drawing room; he was camouflaged against the furnishings in the dim light but as his figure emerged, I held out my hand: 'Hullo, father, I'm back. Your son, Cedric' I took the small pulpy hand in mine; I could feel the bones under the envelope of flesh.

These moments begin to contract, however. My childhood is stretched like a sheet in front of me; it is all around me, too, like the closed doors of the five children's rooms. I traded mine with Joyce when she told me she couldn't stand the view any longer. Father had determinedly put her beside the window. Yes, he and Mary were out hunting when we made the move secretly. I remember her sick quilted face with the eiderdown up to her chin; wilful in spite of the pillage of tuberculosis, she became a Catholic in final defiance of death. But nothing worked. The old Protestant spoilsport ethic seeped into every crevice of the house. When the parish priest passed father on the stairs they neither of them acknowledged each other. It was only when father was out thereafter that the house was able to stretch itself and the priest's voice could be heard from every room like a swarm of bees.

I remember my father once coming out of Joyce's room; I had the wireless full on at the time—Mantovani playing an arrangement of *Goodnight Vienna*—when there was an astonishing noise on the landing. A huge gulping sound like the plug being pulled out of the bath. My curiosity drove me to peep out of the door and there was father in full hunting rigout, sobbing. He had his back to me and the sea-green jacket had a tinsel streak down the back—a trick of the light from the north window.

He must have acknowledged Death as no man's master. His daughter's relaxation in grace, to him, must have simply been a defeatist attitude.

Yes. Those were my tangled thoughts that wild autumn night the day my father died. What happened later is even more confusing.

When I went back into the drawing room I perceived that my father was having an attack of some kind. He was writhing in his chair, his face had become purple. My mother had risen and was standing over him, not reaching out to him, but holding in one hand a small elephant bell which she rolled over and over, hoping no doubt that the tinny peels would attract the attention of Theresa or myself. I shoved her out of the way and tore open the old man's shirt; his brittle breastbone seemed to pierce the skin with his effort to draw in air. I took him in my arms and raced back upstairs with him and, laying him on his bed, I covered him up. Luckily there was an extension to the telephone by his side.

All the time while I heard the brr … brr … I was conscious of the wind outside banging against the wall, making the copper beech groan with each blast; confusedly I talked to the doctor, explained who I was. Yes, right away, he'd come.

There was a strange calciferous smell in the room, which I couldn't identify. The parsimonious bedside lamp cast such a dim light that the room seemed to sway in its shadows. There were bookshelves, too, lining both walls. But I had to keep an uneasy eye on father, trapped as I was in the approach of his unheroic death. As a child I had believed that all old men were heroes, but sitting there beside him I saw no hero, just a poor old tyrant taking his last few lungfuls of air. From time to time I thought he was going to say something and I bent my ear close to his lips in the hope that some last tenderness might come forth. But the effort was beyond him. Just before the end he opened his mouth and a little water ran out and settled on the pillow-case. I closed the jaw; he was dead.

Looking back on it now it seems to me that for a few seconds after his death I became my father. I was conscious of a feeling of tremendous pride, or perhaps satisfaction is a better word. I was walking up a very steep hill; it was difficult because, although I was leaning forward, every step I took threw the top of my body backwards. The hill wound between two high walls and every few yards there was a shallow step. And it was hot, but not unpleasantly so; a fine breeze touched my cheek and occasionally lifted my hair. At the top of the hill, which I reached at last feeling greatly fatigued, there was a doorway in the wall. I went through this and met, by appointment, my mother. She was young and not unattractive, dressed in a powder blue costume. She held a parasol, tilted slightly backwards over herself and the table she was sitting at. I said in a rather surprised voice: 'You look like a Monet.' I don't think she replied but at any rate I sat down beside her and we both watched two lizards darting over the terracotta walls. Minute particles of sand fell soundlessly as they scraped and clung with their tiny fists. 'They are like my thoughts,' I said.

The unreflective activity of the animals had such a soothing effect on me that I decided then and there I would purchase the house in Killiney I had gone to view before leaving Ireland to go on my honeymoon. The century had just turned the corner and this ripe Italianate residence would be a fitting place to rear my family. My eldest son would be called Cedric after my grandfather, Dr Cedric Stewart, a good man who had refused a knighthood from Queen Victoria on the grounds that he didn't believe he should be honoured for his researches; he devoted his whole life thereafter to tending to the Dublin poor. I called the waiter to pay for my Slivovitz and Edith's citrus drink, but, instead of the waiter, a young plum-skinned girl ran out and took my few coins; I don't think we exchanged words except I do remember the one word: 'Dobre'.

'Good evening, I'm Dr Fitzmaurice,' the restrained tones of the doctor must have brought me back to the present because I found myself staring at the wall beyond father's bed. I had already noticed the bookshelves but now I realised there was something strange about the books; they were all mine. My entire childhood collection thrown together higgledy-piggledy... *The Count of Monte Cristo, Dr Doolittle, The Three Musketeers, The Complete Works of Dickens* ...

'Thank you for coming, I'm afraid it's too late.'

And those of my teens... *Thus Spake Zarathustra, Alice in Wonderland*—Joyce's favourite book ...

'No trouble. There would have been little I could have done.'

... *The Sorrows of Young Werther* ...

'I'll send a woman up from Ballybrack to lay him out.'

... *Gray's Anatomy* ... This must have been Richard's.

'Yes,' the doctor continued. 'He would have wanted you by his side at the end. He spoke often of you. He was very proud of you.'

... Two novels by Evelyn Waugh in Penguin editions ...

'He used to show me your postcards. I believe you are a very distinguished historian, Mr Stewart. You are a lucky man to have seen so much of the world.'

I remember a line of Whitman's:

I am your voice—it was tied in you—in me it begins to talk.

I feel a great blanket of fatigue lying heavily over me.

'Would you like to sit down?' I say, trying to make my muffled tones audible; he has such a kind face, this man, with soft sandy-coloured eyes.

'No, no. I won't trouble you further. You'll have much to do. I think your mother ...'

'Yes. I'll have to go down to her ...'

'You look very tired, Mr Stewart.'

'Perhaps I slept for a moment or two. I'm not sure. Would you mind waiting a min ...'

As I rise—making an effort to control my trembling limbs—I suddenly realise the reason for the calciferous smell. All my marine treasures that I gathered during my solitary walks along the beach are in a box underneath my father's bed— starfish, sponges, fronds of bladder-wrack, sea-mat, periwinkles, limpets, minute cowrie shells—he has kept them all these years ...

'Yes,' I mutter, not properly understanding my own meaning, 'It's just as I thought ...'

The doctor's trim shoulders bob down the stairs in front

of me as he chatters away. 'These old houses, you know. A lot of damp ... of course I like to see them remain in the same family ... It's terrible what's happening in the city, now ... no feeling for the old ...'

Theresa waits for us at the bottom of the stairs. 'Your father, Cedric?'

I take her hand in mine. I am ashamed because I can do nothing to appease our plight; in a few days I shall be gone and her life will flutter away from her like feathers off a little bird; but together, at least, we stand at the moment.

The Quest

WHAT WAS I THINKING ABOUT as I stepped off the train?

A black- (could be called raven-) haired infant?

A baby of about three weeks, a lusty, hungry demanding human being?

So what was this 'Charles'? An elongated baby? Lusty, demanding, never satisfied? One who changes women frequently, drives heavy, expensive cars?

A baby with long shins like a new-born foal.

Called Seán. Simple. Just Seán. No frills or attachments to the distaff side.

Seán then. But now 'Charles'. They changed the name. (And personality?)

And now a thirty-nine-year-old. Tall. Must be tall because of the shins. You can tell at three weeks.

It was a blowy day. Full of gusts, cold for August. There was a hint of cows and running water.

The platform was deserted. A tiny place, like a toy. The kind of station with just one apron, a tub of geraniums, a corrugated awning. To get to the other side one just walked across the line.

All around was England. Strange. I was alert from lack of sleep, everything sharp planes and angles as though the fields and farmhouses could be separated and reset in whatever pattern I wished. Except to the left where a row of houses peeped above trees. A solid row of tiled roofs and tall chimneys.

Twenty past. They mustn't be coming. What had the organisation said? 'You'll probably be met'? *Probably?*

So I wasn't met.

The crumpled piece of paper said, 3 Mill Lane, the village of Crowsfort. Yes, the cruciform legend read 'Crowsfort'.

Plough Monday. He'd been born on Plough Monday. Forty-eight hour labour. Narrow pelvis, they said. Parthenogenesis. No penetration. Peculiar.

We heard the first V2. The nurses had rushed to the window.

'A gas explosion,' they said, resuming their work.

Later, when we knew, we were frightened.

I left the platform, followed the path, found a closed-in lane, a lane bordered with trimmed box-hedge, the pebbles underfoot crunched like biscuit. It curled a little, narrowed, and there was an old fashioned stile into a graveyard.

The church was on the left. It had a Romanesque front, like the belly of a hen, and a short spire. Well, not a spire, really. Something more like the peak of a cap. A complacent little building quietly watching over the lichen-covered tombstones, the long grasses, even the primly landscaped area of more recent interments. Names like Hawsthorne, Towdie and Holmquist, Broadbent, Fairchild and one Smith, some sort of chief, he must have been, because many of his forebears were listed on the high memorial—a granite needle which raced skywards, baring their souls to the angels.

Afterwards there had been papers to sign. Yes, a very well-to-do couple. Educated and cultured also. He'll have a wonderful life. And I hadn't shed a tear. They expected me to cry. No. The long trauma was over. In three weeks I would be seventeen. And free.

Beyond the churchyard the vista opened up and I was in a road deep in chestnut trees. The houses to one side were quaint, pseudo-Elizabethan, with dormer windows that opened on a hinge, and curtains billowing out like different coloured tongues. At the end of the road I could see cars parked higgledy-piggledy with young women disgorging, calling to each other. Tiny children, pretty as butterflies, were being gathered up. They held out their offerings, plasticine figurines, dolls made from toilet rolls, pipe-cleaner animals, drawings in chalk.

As I neared them I could hear them talking. 'Say goodbye to Lena, Jenny, Paul.' 'Come on, Cherry, you'll see Austen tomorrow,' and Austen with a big black howl coming out of his stomach.

'Where is Mill Lane?' I asked a woman, a pretty, down-to-earth woman of about twenty-eight. She called out, 'Mill Lane, Peg? Know where Mill Lane is?'

No. No one knew Mill Lane. 'Must be the other side of town. You could ask in there. She's lived here all her life.'

She pointed to the only sad house. The house that needed paint, the garden that needed flowers.

I knocked. A voice called down from a window, 'Is that Rosie?'

'No,' I called back.

She appeared. A vexed face, uncared for as her garden.

Thought you was Rosie.'

'Sorry. It's just...' She dragged me in. It was dim. She wheezed a little. 'What you want?'

'Please. I'm disturbing you. I only wanted to know...'

'This way.'

There was an absence of symmetry or sense to the room.

Settees and stools, all balding velvet, and old gold ruche, glass-topped tables, ornaments ... Little blackmen in boats, gondolas, Hansel and Gretel houses, a cuckoo clock and a shepherd and shepherdess in filigree plastic.

'About time you come back.' Her hair looped down from a dusty ribbon. Dyed and dry as grass with the giveaway line of grey at the roots, it gave her lined face an operatic sadness, the melancholy of the ageing prima donna who goes for her last audition.

Agile as a grasshopper, she kneed aside the furnishing as she cut through the labyrinth, extracting a bottle—unmarked—from a sideboard near the fireplace.

"Ere luv.' She held out a tumbler, pouring one for herself. Neat gin.

I let it in slowly. We both stood. Stared.

'3 Mill Lane,' I said. 'Could you direct me?'

'So you come back,' she repeated.

'Sorry. I'm not Rosie. Nan. Nan MacDonald. Looking for ... a friend.'

'Ill go on,' I added. 'Won't disturb you any longer. Thank you for the drink.'

'You can't fool me.' My wrist in her hand felt the bones under the flesh, wobbling, silky like the skin of a frog. My business was elsewhere. Who was Rosie?

'So you'll leave me again?' She dropped my wrist, sat back in her chair, the thin arm holding the drink, the only thing that mattered then. 'Go, then.'

He had lain in a crib with a falciform awning. All pleated organdie, baby-blue, round the edges. That's what they sent to fetch him in. And boy did his dark eyes twirl and twirl and his small fists curl at the end of his long arms. His body was hard as a rock when he bawled and his face screwed up like a bitten apple.

I didn't go to him when he cried. Not always. Sometimes I picked him up and brushed his forehead with my lips if he quietened down. That's during the few weeks in the home. Miss Charity got angry when I lifted him. 'Leave them alone between feeds.' But I couldn't stand the racket. Although the Irish skivvy agreed with me. Grey and toothless as a herring, she'd reared ten, she said, 'And never let a one of them cry.'

The outside world hit me like a sheet, a grey sheet, billowing and blinding me. Breath came in and out as I ran, scorched my chest. I was in the main street. A street of closed shops, windows of flame in the evening sun. Snug grocers and fishmongers, hardware stores and old curiosity shops. Behind one window, velveteen dolls and bouncy balls and a marionette with bunches of golden hair and a Monroe pout hung in her complicated strings one arm lifted, one toe pointed as for a *pas de deux*. Her green tutu struck out each side like a miniature lampshade. At the end of the street, The Crown, a magnificent structure, with carriage lamps and gleaming oak doors, welcomed all comers with a warm smell of hops.

I went in.

They didn't let me meet the couple. It wasn't allowed then. They reassured me once more. When he had gone I played the tinny piano, a waltz by Chopin, a two-part *Invention* by Bach (The one in F major) until I was scolded and stopped. I wandered around. Snow had begun to patter outside. Soft stars on the window-pane. I pressed my nose against the glass, wanting to kiss and feel the clean cold on my lips. The building was cold and damp, a long hall with a refectory table. A table where we ate—all the fallen women—gabbling together, telling each other's story till we knew them off by heart. But it was empty then, no tin plates or cutlery, no clatter. Just the echoing of my steps on the stone floor.

I had to wait three days before I was released with an envelope in which a note said I was fit for work.

The beer took the taste of gin from my mouth. Middle-aged men greeted each other. The barmen called them 'Guv,' and treated all with cordial assurance. It had been a long coming. I was anxious. Someone told me where Mill Lane was. I ordered another beer.

I watched each man in turn. Could one be this 'Charles'? He had sent for me. He was expecting me, wanted to see me. Why, after so long? What had I agreed to come? I remembered 'Rosie'. That woman had expected Rosie, had thought I was Rosie. How long had she waited for Rosie? What had it to do with me?

The beer cooled my thoughts, blunted my nerve ends. Soon I would get up and go to Mill Lane.

The blood drained from me.

Charles had walked into the pub.

I ran to the ladies room, surprised I didn't look too awful, washed my face and hands, combed my hair, put on earrings, adjusted my black coat slightly off my shoulders, belt dangling, to appear casual, collected.

'Is that Charles?'

The man lifted his pint and put it on my table.

He was like my father, loose, dark, thick-browed, six foot perhaps. 'Nan,' he said. 'I knew you at once.' He looked at me oddly. I had said to my father, I'm going to England to work. He had looked at me oddly.

We walked in the dark, following the ball of orange light cast by his torch. I could feel grass underfoot eventually, his voice was amiable. He said he had just moved in, had been expecting me all evening, that his house was one of three tied cottages, and of course the mill had long since fallen into disuse.

'My parents bought this as a country retreat, but sadly never used it.' For once there was a mordant touch to his tones.

They had been killed in an accident last year, he told me.

Inside, two tiny rooms sloped to either side of the narrow hall. They were both empty of furniture except in one a few canvases were stacked against the wall facing inwards.

He stood tall in the bright, friendly, I thought beautiful, his dark hair waving over his sallow brow glowed blue like a crow's wing. 'I'll get two chairs,' he said.

Did he want me now his parents were dead? Uneasily I glanced at the backs of the canvases. What was he? A painter?

He brought food and plates of salad, interpreted my wonderings, said he had left his job to live here, had worked, oh yes for his 'pater'—a splendid man, botanist, scholar—his mother also, now he would retire permanently here. 'In the daylight you'll see it, it's infectious, you'll never want to leave it.' But … but …

Perhaps I learnt something of his ways as he talked, poking here and there into minor episodes of his childhood, schooldays, university.

'I lived with a girl for a while. We couldn't marry. Her husband refused to divorce her, threatened to take her child.'

He'd had no child of his own, no. They'd parted wishy-washy. Was he too good to be true? Too beautiful, too self-contained. Something niggled me. The dark must be there somewhere. The pictures? What was in the pictures?

The fact that I was famous didn't seem to bother him. He knew, remarked lightly he had read about me. (My most recent concert had been in Leningrad, had caused a stir, was widely covered.) It grew late. I asked about the canvases.

'I only paint to find out.' He turned the first. A view of Wicklow. Unmistakable. The big Sugarloaf the backdrop to the purples and browns of heather, bog; a ramshackle cottage, the centrepiece.

I had not thought of him as an artist of any kind. Not even a temptingly bad artist. This daub, so carefully copied from a photograph (probably), must be part of the dark side I was expecting he would expose sooner or later.

'Yes, I know,' he said seeing my look of consternation. 'It's awful, isn't it.'

'It's not so much that.' I was stuck for words.

'I copied it from a picture postcard.'

'Are the others all famous Irish views?' I asked limply.

'No. Worse. They are of women. Or rather one woman.' He let out a long breath like an 'AAAH', making no effort to turn the pictures round.

We sat for a while in silence. Although he had talked sporadically about himself, he made no effort to ask about my life. Time didn't seem to belong to him. Between babyhood and his fortieth year no time seemed to have passed at all. His life had been led in a field of shadows. My presence here was simply another shadow that would pass, leaving yet more shadows of a greyer hue.

The fire spat and flamed and he had sat down again and leant slightly forward, elbows on knees, hands occasionally stretched towards the heat. I found it uncomfortably warm and pushed my chair away. Then he got up. 'I'll show you,' he said.

One by one he turned the pictures round. The first was clearly a self-portrait, that is to say of a woman resembling himself. She had the same dark features and continental skin, the same narrow face and neat head. But there was something missing. The expression was empty, like one who is heavily drugged. The second somewhat similar except that he had tried to thicken the paint to give the impression of the ageing of the skin. The last two were increasingly horrific. Here the artist began to show some genuine talent—or if not talent,

116

imagination—although once again they were clichés. The final picture, especially. In this she was represented as an old hag, the conventional witch, the epitome of evil.

He stood behind it now, glaring at me. 'You see I had to find out. They tried to shelter me, pampered me, gave in to my whims. They emptied me there.' He tapped his forehead.

'I didn't send for you until I'd finished this last one,' he continued.

It was as though he were trying to emulate evil, the evil he had tried to portray. The face had changed from polite to sour, the childish pout on his lips reminded me of the marionette in the window of the shop. He left the canvas and went into the kitchen, swaggering somewhat as he passed me.

Should I creep away, I wondered. But I didn't move, sat as though sculpted, another of his effigies. Didn't move until he came slowly out, the light dancing on the long blade of the kitchen knife, and then I jumped to my feet, backed against the wall, making myself an easier target if anything. But while he waved the knife in my direction he immediately began to hack at the canvas, tearing it across and across until finally he ripped it off its frame and threw it into the fire. Shreds of hair went chasing up the chimney and he stood and watched until the last ragged piece had faded into ash.

'Upon such sacrifices, my Cordelia, the gods themselves throw incense.' Did I say that out loud? I'm not sure. Anyway he went on staring into the fire. The logs had begun to die down, the black ash had quelled the flames, he kicked a piece of wood and a few sparks lifted to subside immediately. He turned to me. 'I told you, I just wanted to find out.'

'And have you?'

He made a metronomic movement with his head, his expression a melancholic void.

I picked up my bag.

'It's all in the travelling,' I said. 'Goodbye.'

I may have added, I'm booked into The Crown, or, if you're in Ireland, look me up.

I can't remember.